T0209557

SECOND EDITION

HOME SWEET WELL MANAGED HOME

ESSENTIALS OF HOUSEHOLD MANAGEMENT

EDWIN B. EMERY JR.

WESTBOW
PRESS®
A DIVISION OF THOMAS NELSON
& ZONDERVAN

WestBow Press books may be ordered through booksellers or by contacting:

WestBow Press
A Division of Thomas Nelson & Zondervan
1663 Liberty Drive
Bloomington, IN 47403
www.westbowpress.com
844-714-3454

Scripture quotations taken from The Holy Bible, New International Version® NIV® Copyright © 1973 1978 1984 2011 by Biblica, Inc. TM. Used by permission. All rights reserved worldwide.

ISBN: 978-1-6642-2006-5 (sc)
ISBN: 978-1-6642-2007-2 (e)

Library of Congress Control Number: 2021901570

Print information available on the last page.

WestBow Press rev. date: 04/30/2021

CONTENTS

PREFACE

This book includes descriptions of the basic essentials of household management. Addressed herein are various aspects of security, safety, budgets, files, insurance, living trusts, planning, health, maintenance, investing, and essentials of a personal nature. For the most part, this book is written in summary form so that the reader can save time and get straight to the heart of the matter.

This book is chock-full of good concepts, ideas, specific techniques, detailed examples, and useful blank work sheets. All of these have been tried and proven over a period of many years and may be relied upon to provide excellent household management results. Buy this book and try these ideas – you'll like them.

For the most part, this writing excludes the subject of interpersonal relationships. Also, you will not find a hundred pages of explanations of whys and wherefores. Rather, the author trusts that the reader will recognize and use the good common sense ideas presented here.

The full size pages were selected for this book to permit the easy reproduction of 8½" X 11" forms.

I would like to express my sincere gratitude to the Sunrise Secretarial Company for typing this manuscript, to my wife Patricia for her editorial help, and to my good friend Bonnie for her financial assistance.

CHAPTER 1

ESSENTIALS OF HOUSEHOLD SECURITY

SECURITY EVALUATION
SECURITY EQUIPMENT
THEFT OF PERSONAL IDENTIFICATION
MAIL THEFT
ACTIONS TO REDUCE HOUSEHOLD THEFT

ESSENTIALS OF HOUSEHOLD SECURITY

Security Evaluation

Start with a careful evaluation of your dwelling security risks. Some police and sheriffs departments have representatives who can provide you with some crime statistics and otherwise help you with your security evaluation. Some will meet with you to provide information specifically applicable to you, to help organize neighborhood watch programs, and to make security suggestions.

Security Equipment

After this risk evaluation is made, acquire adequate security systems to protect you and your home. In a quiet suburban area that experiences little or no crime, a simple system of two or three motion detectors, a control panel, and a smoke detector might be sufficient for your home. In a high crime rate area or to protect high-value assets, you will need some of the following security equipment:

1. Motion detectors covering all dwelling areas.
2. Alarm circuits for each window and each perimeter pedestrian door and for under-carpet pressure pads.
3. Metal bars for each window and each perimeter door.
4. Outside flood lights (usually turned on automatically at twilight).
5. Outside motion-activated surveillance cameras.
6. Motion-activated dummy surveillance cameras.
7. Auto entry gate with key or push button locking system.
8. Automatic emergency light machines or an electrical generator.
9. Heavy steel combination-lock fire proof safe.
10. Robbery or panic push-button alarm system for life threatening situations.
11. For travel, a portable electromagnetic security system or door knob burglar alarm.
12. Wired or wireless driveway motion sensor and monitor.
13. Solid perimeter doors at least 1.75 inches thick. Hollow doors are not secure and can be easily kicked down.
14. For all perimeter doors, use a deadbolt lock. The key-in-knob lock set is not secure.
15. For windows that adjoin exterior doors, use shatter-resistant polycarbonate.
16. Timers to operate lights, radios, and other electrical devices when you are away on a trip. These can be programmed to turn on and off at any time of the day or night as needed.
17. Garage door remote control that changes the remote's code after each use.

18. Small signs on windows and perimeter doors saying that you have an alarm system – whether or not you have one.

19. Use a sign that says "Beware of Dog" that is visible from the street – whether or not you have a dog.

Some cities and counties require a permit before an alarm system may be installed. Some charge a service fee for false alarms.

For added security, you may wish to obtain the services of a central monitoring company. This service requires a monitoring agreement for a specified period of time and for a monthly fee. It also requires that someone turn on the monitoring service each time you want this type of protection when the dwelling is unoccupied, and then it requires that someone turn off this alarm service when reentry is made. Some systems provide for periphery doors and windows protection while the dwelling is occupied.

With the installation of an alarm system, a certificate of installation should be obtained. Such a certificate, when sent to your insurance company or agent, may entitle you to a discount in your home owners insurance.

Theft of Personal Identification

Theft of personal identification, especially by computer users, is becoming an increasing problem. Identity theft is the cause of many complex problems and may result in your worst financial nightmare. There are several steps to take to avoid this type of theft:

1. Make certain that you are receiving bank account and credit card statements and that you are receiving them on time. If these statements aren't showing up, it could mean that someone has stolen your identity. Review your statements for unauthorized activity.

2. Do not throw away any document that includes such personal information as your social security, drivers license, bank account, or credit card account numbers. Rather, buy a paper shredder and use it to dispose of throw-away documents that contain any personal numbers.

3. Carefully guard your personal information and provide it only when necessary to do so and only when you are certain that it is appropriate. When necessary for purchases or for other valid reasons, provide credit card numbers by using land-line phones only – do not use cordless phones.

4. At least twice a year, obtain a copy of your credit report from any of the national credit report companies. Review it for accuracy and, if there are errors, fill out the proper form to obtain corrections.

At the time of this writing, there were three National Credit Organizations (consumer reporting agencies):

Equifax

Experian

Trans Union

The credit reports issued by these organizations include a file number, your Social Security number, other personal information, all your charge account numbers with amounts charged and paid and the credit limits, bank loan numbers with the balances owed and payments made, and a list of all companies that requested and received a copy of your credit report. Needless to say, all copies of this report should be stored in a locked file cabinet and should be shredded before being discarded.

You have a wide range of rights under both federal and state Fair Credit Reporting Acts. An explanation of these rights is included with each copy of your credit report. You should read about and make use of these rights.

5. Do not share your telephone access code or Personalized Identification Number (PIN) with anyone and don't carry them in your wallet or purse.
6. Closely limit the number of credit cards and pieces of identification you carry, and store your Social Security Card and Birth Certificate in a secure file.
7. Because of extra security features, order your checks through your bank, make certain each order is accurate and complete.
8. Immediately report lost or stolen checks, charge cards, compromised PINs and passwords to the issuing agency.
9. Do not preprint your driver's license or Social Security numbers on your checks.
10. Every time you use a point-of-sale terminal or ATM, shield the keypad when you enter your PIN, and make sure to take your transaction receipt with you.
11. When using your charge card for purchases, always check your sales slip to verify the correct amount has been entered before completing the transaction, and always take your receipt with you.
12. For additional information on guarding your identity, write to the Federal Trade Commission or visit it's web site.

Mail Theft

Mail theft might also be a problem (can be terrible and time-consuming), and steps should be taken to protect your mail.

1. For incoming mail: with an outside, unlocked box, pick up the mail as soon as possible after its delivery; use a lockable mail box; use a mail slot wherein the delivered mail drops inside the house or garage and is out of reach from the outside; or use a rental box at a post office or postal substation. While on a trip, stop all mail deliveries.
2. For outgoing mail: take it to a post office; drop it into an in-use postal service drop box; or take it to a postal substation.
3. Some increased security may be obtained by converting your paper checks to electronic checks for use in making purchases and for paying bills by using a computer.

Actions to Reduce Household Theft

Make your home less attractive to thieves by following a few simple steps:

1. Before you leave your dwelling, lock all outside doors (use a safety bar on sliding glass doors) and close all drapes, opaque curtains, and blinds.
2. Before you go to bed, close and lock all windows except for those absolutely needed for ventilation.
3. Don't leave keys in secret hiding places near or outside your perimeter doors. Burglars know all these places.
4. Keep all garage doors closed and locked. Use your garage for your auto/s and, secondly, as a work and storage area.
5. While you are out of town, make certain that newspapers and other deliveries are collected each day.
6. When on vacation or other trip for longer than a few days, arrange for someone to take care of your yard work or to clear snow off the walks and driveway.
7. Make a joint effort with your neighbors to immediately report to the police anything suspicious in your neighborhood. Set up a neighborhood watch program, including signs and window stickers, with the guidance of your local police.
8. Keep the area under windows clear of bushes that are tall enough to hide the windows.
9. The fewer people you tell about a planned trip, the better. Make certain that no stranger hears about your plans.

CHAPTER 2

ESSENTIALS OF HOUSEHOLD SAFETY

ESSENTIAL SAFETY DOs
ESSENTIAL SAFETY DON'Ts

ESSENTIALS OF HOUSEHOLD SAFETY

In everything, think and put safety first. Each year millions of Americans sustain household-accident injuries. The following recommendations will help you reduce the risk of such injuries (and possibly prevent deaths):

Essential Safety DOs

1. Learn about the causes and prevention of home fires. Good sources of information are your insurance and utility companies. Make certain that there are both smoke and carbon monoxide detectors in place and working. Have fire-extinguishing equipment installed—manually operated extinguishers or perhaps a completely automatic sprinkler system. Develop an escape plan and make sure that everyone living in the household knows about it. Know the location of gas and electric meters and how to shut them off in an emergency. Know how to safely operate furnaces, space heaters, ranges, and water heaters; and have them inspected by a licensed contractor at least annually.

   Install single or multi-station smoke detectors as needed. In single story households, install detectors in hallways outside the bedroom areas. In a household with two or more stories, install multi-station smoke detectors on each floor in such a way that they are interconnected, i.e., alarms on an upper floor would sound if an alarm sounds on a lower floor. Test alarms regularly, and if battery operated, change batteries every six months.

   There are several types of manually operated fire extinguishers: water base agent, regular dry chemical, multi-purpose dry chemical, carbon dioxide gas, etc. You should become familiar with the uses and limitations of each type. The multi-purpose dry chemical is the best choice for general use in the household.

   Purchase only fire-resistant draperies, curtains, carpets, upholstery, children's clothing, and roofing materials. Maintain a thirty-foot wide space around your house as a defensible fire barrier. Keep the exhaust pipe of the clothes dryer free of lint.

   Trim dead limbs hanging over a house or garage and cut back all tree limbs within fifteen feet of a chimney. Install properly designed screens over all air ducts and chimneys. Use glass doors or screens in front of all fireplaces. An advantage of glass doors is that they can shut off air to quench the fire before retiring. Of course, the fireplace damper should always be opened before lighting a fire.

In the kitchen, install a smoke detector and change the batteries at six month intervals. Have a fire extinguisher and baking soda near the stove to extinguish stovetop fires. Keep potholders, curtains, loose clothing, and other flammable materials at a safe distance from stove burners. Spilled grease on top of stove, in the oven, and under burners should be wiped up immediately since it is a fire hazard. Make sure that stove exhaust fans and ducts are free of dust and grease buildup.

If you smell leaking utility gas, open nearby windows and, to avoid an explosion, refrain from switching on lights or striking a match. Shut off main gas supply valve at the meter, vacate the house at once and, from a neighbor's house or by cell phone, call the fire department and local gas company. Furnaces, boilers, and water heaters must be properly vented to the outside. Your water heater must be equipped with a temperature relief valve.

Heating and air conditioning systems, refrigerator, and freezer coils should be cleaned and serviced regularly––at least annually. Fireplace chimneys should be periodically cleaned and inspected for cracks.

To escape a fire, stay low to the floor, where the best air collects, and always roll out of bed rather than sit or stand straight up. To prevent a rush of air currents into a room, close the doors before opening any windows. If a closed door feels hot to the touch leave it closed and find another way out. In upstairs bedrooms keep rope ladders easily available––they could save your life.

2. Keep on hand emergency supplies including a battery-operated radio, bottled water (rotate every four months), a flashlight, candles, matches, a manually operated can opener, a first aid kit, a wind-up or battery operated clock, and, if you have a fireplace, fire wood ready for use.
3. If there is an electrical power outage: notify your power supplier company; turn off all electrical appliances; and leave one light switch on so that it will be obvious when power is restored. Avoid going near any downed power line.
4. Keep alcoholic drinks, cleaners, sprays, bleach, etc. out of reach of children. For these items, install a lockable storage cabinet at a height that is out of reach of children.
5. Keep guns locked up and, if you own a gun, make certain that all members of the household receive instructions about gun safety.
6. Operate electrical appliances such as radios, televisions, hair dryers, and the like away from any water––especially bath tubs and showers. Make certain that the area around washing machines and dryers is clean and dry. The combination of electricity and water can be deadly. The same is true of electric extension cords. Replace cords that are broken, frayed, or that have melted or burned parts.
7. When cooking, keep children a safe distance away from the stove. Each year, children are horribly burned and disfigured from hot liquids spilled from stove tops.

8. Water heaters should be anchored to wall studs to prevent them from tipping over and breaking gas and water lines. In an emergency, water in the tank can be saved for drinking.

9. If you smell or suspect a gas leak, shut off the main gas meter until the leak is stopped. Refrain from using matches and electrical switches in the gas leak area. Use a flashlight for this purpose. While the leak is being fixed, open windows and doors and get everyone out of the building.

10. If any project requires the digging of a hole of any significant depth, call your utility companies to obtain information about the location of buried lines. An example would be the installation or replacement of sewer drain pipes.

11. For any heavy or prolonged lifting, use a good back support to prevent injuries. When possible, bend your knees when you lift rather than your back.

12. Use eye protection when working around flying pieces of metal, wood, plastic, or other chips and when working in a dusty area. Well-fitting safety goggles or safety glasses are essential. For welding, save your eyesight by wearing a good quality welding helmet (never look at a welding flame without eye protection.) Always have a clean eye wash cup readily available.

13. For ear protection from loud or continuous noises such as those made by yard clean-up blowers, use close-fitting ear muffs, ear bands, or foam ear plugs.

14. There are several types of gloves available to protect your hands from toxic and other chemicals and in performing manual work. Included are gloves that are chemical resistant, coated work, cotton work, cut resistant, heat resistant, impregnated, leather, rubber, welding, and yard. Use the correct glove for each application.

15. Of course it is very important to protect your head from injury. The most common type of injury is falling from a recreational vehicle such as a bicycle, skateboard, motorcycle, roller skates, or ice skates. Use helmets, hard hats, bump caps, face shields, or visors as required for each applicable activity. Some states have passed laws requiring the use of protective head gear.

16. Assembled respirators, disposable respirators, full pace pieces, and half-mask face pieces are available for lung protection in areas contaminated with dust, fumes, particles, and other contaminants.

17. There are several ways to help control infections in the home. Wash your hands frequently with soap and water, when reentering your dwelling after a trip – especially after handling money. Cover all coughs and sneezes with a handkerchief or disposable tissue. With disinfectant, periodically clean all household handles: door, cupboards, faucets, etc.

18. If you have a swimming pool, closely adhere to all local ordinances pertaining to pool safety. Use high fences and a locked gate to prevent unsupervised children from entering the pool area. All poolside areas should have nonskid surfaces.

19. Working on a roof requires special precautions. Use shoes with non-slip soles. To prevent falling off, use safety ropes, even if it requires another person to hold the rope, and ladders with gripper hooks or safety bars. When possible, work from the ground – for example, when cleaning rain gutters – rather than the roof.

20. When hauling anything in an open-bed truck, always use tie down ropes or other types of lanyards.

21. Avoid the serious illness caused by food poisoning. Eat only clean foods that you know are not spoiled or contaminated.

22. When an electrical circuit is overloaded or develops a short, a fuse blows or a circuit breaker trips – whichever you have. When this happens, find and fix the problem and then replace the fuse with a new one or flip the circuit breaker switch to the "on" position. It may be necessary to firmly press this switch to the "off" position first then flip it firmly to the "on" position. If you cannot find the cause, call an electrician.

23. If an extension cord must be used, make certain that the cord wire size is thick enough for its length and intended load. For most household applications, cord gauge sizes from ten to eighteen are adequate.

24. Use the original, labeled containers for all household chemicals so that mistakes in their use will be avoided. When empty, rinse and discard containers.

25. If any wax is used on floors, use the nonskid type and wipe up all spills immediately.

26. Sink, stove, and other working areas should be well lighted.

27. When cooking, always turn pot handles away from the front of the stove, but not over another hot burner.

28. Use the proper slotted storage racks, even inside drawers, for sharp knives.

29. To prevent falls, use a strong, safe step stool rather than makeshift substitutes.

30. Make certain that all small rugs have a nonskid backing.

31. On large glass areas – sliding doors and floor to ceiling windows – use decals or streamers to prevent anyone from mistaking them for door openings.

32. Only buy high quality toys that match the age of your children. Use very conservative judgement to avoid toys that can be swallowed, that can cut, that involve fumes or powders and, importantly, provide adequate space in which to use the toys. Also provide adequate storage and insist that children put away toys when they are finished playing with them.

33. When needed, repair broken pedestrian surfaces such as floors, stairs, driveways, and walkways. Keep these areas well lighted.

34. Keep weeds, grasses, and all other combustibles away from areas around fences, stairways, and under porches.

35. After using them, return all yard tools and equipment to their proper storage area and racks.

36. Always keep small children a safe distance from all swings while they are not in the swings.

37. Stairways should be built with sturdy handrails, banisters, and close-together upright supports. They should be well lighted with three-way switches at both the bottom and the top. Keep treads and carpeting in good repair. Keep stairways clear of throw rugs, toys, and other items.

38. Make certain that all bathroom and closet doors can be opened from the inside.

39. Upstairs window sills should be at least three feet from the floor, or the windows should be covered with protective bars.

40. Make sure that clothing does not touch closet light bulbs.

41. Keep all flammable items a safe distance from electric baseboards and other heaters.

42. Keep cosmetics away from children including those kept in purses.

43. When not in use, disconnect power tools and store them. Keep all tools out of reach of children.

44. Flammable liquids should be stored in their original containers at a safe distance from the pilot lights of water heaters and the furnace.

45. Oily rags should be stored in air-tight metal cans.

46. Use only appliances and power tools that bear the "UL" label. The same is true for Christmas lights.
47. Immediately turn off any appliance or power tool that sparks, stalls or overheats, and have it repaired before using it again.
48. Disconnect your iron and put it on its stand if you leave your ironing board for more than a minute or two.
49. Keep paper, cloths, and other flammables a safe distance from light bulbs.

Essential Safety Don'ts

1. Don't smoke in the house. However, if you can't manage that, do not smoke while you are in a reclining position and never smoke while you are lying down.
2. When cooking, don't leave the stove area when stove burners are turned on high.
3. Never use an open flame heater indoors for example, a portable propane heater.
4. Don't overload electrical outlets. Never allow children to play with electrical outlets and don't forget to put safety covers over unused outlets.
5. Avoid any contact with overhead power lines – especially with ladders, poles, kites, model airplanes, antennas, tree trimmers, etc.
6. Never back up any vehicle without first walking around in back of it to be certain that the intended path is clear and, especially, that there is no child or pet in harms way (some older pets are deaf).
7. Do not come in contact with the saliva of any household pet. Any pet bite or scratch, even if small, should be thoroughly washed with antibacterial soap and then disinfected. If red streaks appear on the skin near the bite or scratch, do not hesitate to get medical attention immediately.
8. Never touch a metal object connected to the ground, such as a faucet, while touching a plugged in electrical appliance.
9. If a basement or room is flooded, never enter these areas without turning off all household electrical circuits. If you do, you may be electrocuted.
10. Unless you first turn off the circuit, never throw water on an electrical fire.
11. Never use a major appliance unless it is grounded with a three-wire plug.
12. Make certain that there are no electrical switches or outlets within reach of a sink, shower, or bathtub.
13. Do not locate walkways near ground floor windows that open outward.
14. Do not swim alone and, in your swimming pool, do not allow your children, relatives or others to do so. Never leave a child in or around a swimming pool, even for a minute or two. Keep all pets out of the pool.
15. Never keep sleeping pills or other medicines on bedside nightstands.
16. Do not install an outside antenna without providing a ground connection.
17. Do not have a television set on while no one is watching.
18. Never leave appliances running while you are away from them. This includes washers, dryers, and dishwashers.

19. Do not leave the area of a plugged-in heating device that does not have its own thermostatic control.
20. Never leave candles burning unattended, never use real candles on a Christmas tree.
21. Do not place a Christmas tree near a heat source such as a fireplace, radiator, television set, etc.
22. Do not plant trees high in oil and resins within twenty feet from your house.
23. Except when driving in or out, do not run an automobile engine in the garage and, certainly, not in an enclosed one.

CHAPTER 3

ESSENTIAL HOUSEHOLD BUDGET OF CASH, EXPENSES, AND INCOME

BUDGET FORMAT
CASH BUDGETING
RECURRING EXPENSE BUDGETING
VARIABLE EXPENSE BUDGETING
ESTIMATED INCOME BUDGETING
LEDGER OF ACTUAL EXPENSE PAYMENTS
BUDGET CONCEPT ADVANTAGES
PROCEDURES FOR USE OF CASH AND PAYMENT OF EXPENSES

ESSENTIAL HOUSEHOLD BUDGET OF CASH, EXPENSES, AND INCOME

1. Budgeting Format

Prepare a budget using the format shown in Example 3-1. In early November of each year, prepare a budget for each month, January through June, of the following year. For example, in November 2003, prepare a monthly budget for the first half of 2004. Similarly, in early May of each year prepare a budget for each month, July through December, of the same year. In each such budget, include monthly amounts for the following separate items:

Cash
Recurring Expenses
Total of Cash and Recurring Expenses
Variable Expenses
Unassigned Reserve
Spendable Income

The objectives of this budgeting system are several:

A. It provides adequate financial information with the expenditure of a small amount of time and effort. To attempt to budget in smaller increments, such as for food, gasoline, clothing, etc., is not only inaccurate but also time consuming and cumbersome. It is too difficult to accumulate actual expenditures with which to compare budgeted amounts.
B. If a carefully prepared budget is followed, the expenditure of household monies is easily controlled.
C. Overuse of credit accounts is easily evident and easily prevented.
D. Financial planning and payment flexibility are vital advantages with this budgeting system.

2. Cash Budgeting

The cash budget should be the estimated amount required to pay for all cash expenditures described in the Section <u>Procedures for Use of Cash and for Payment of Expenses</u>. In the budget form, separate budget amounts should be shown for cash for the first half of each month and for cash for the last half of each month as shown in Example 3-1. For the first two or three months, trial amounts of cash should be budgeted. To establish the realistic cash budget amount, it would be helpful to collect all the bills and sales slips for significant items such as food/restaurant and gasoline for a month, and then add them to find the total amount actually spent. Thereafter, the budgeted cash amount should remain relatively constant – at least until changing household circumstances require a change.

The cash budget should be established very carefully since it is one of the critical factors used to systematically control the prudent use of household monies. The convenience of using cash for many purchases is easy to understand, and furthermore, it avoids the necessity of frequent visits to an ATM with its associated fees. Also, it eliminates the need to write checks for low-value purchases.

3.   Recurring Expense Budgeting

Using the budget form, prepare a monthly budget for each item of recurring expense as shown in Example 3-1. Include those expenses the payment of which is expected to continue for an extended period of time. Included would be such items as mortgage loans, auto loans, property taxes, telephone, etc. The monthly amount to be budgeted for each item should be based on actual expenditures recorded in the Ledger of Actual Expense Payments (see Example 3-2) and adjusted for any known or anticipated changes. For the first year of monthly budgets, the estimated amounts should be based on paid amounts recorded in the checking account checkbook register. Each budget amount should be rounded upward to the nearest $10. For example, an expected payment of $114 should be budgeted at $120.

Where possible, such as for utilities, the use of level-type monthly payment amounts results in more accurate budgets and is, therefore, more valuable in the over all control of expenditures. Of course, not all expenses will be budgeted for each month since some items will occur on a periodic basis. Nevertheless, include these items as recurring expenses if they occur on a regular and predictable schedule. Examples are auto and home insurance, property taxes, quarterly estimated income tax payments, auto registration, and water. On this budget form, check off each item when it is paid. The contingency budget amount will vary with each household. It is used to cover possible expenses that exceed the budgeted amounts or overlooked fixed expense items.

4.   Total of Cash and Recurring Expenses

This monthly total of cash and recurring expenses, when subtracted from the monthly income amount, shows the amount available for payments of variable expenses. This total is also used to calculate the financial position at any given time (see Example 3-4, Calculation of Household Financial Position).

5.   Variable Expense Budgeting

In the budget form, prepare a monthly budget for each significant item of variable expense as shown in Example 3-1. If the payment for an item is expected to remain relatively constant, budget that amount for each month. For example, the item Savings, the item Investment or a credit card item might remain fairly constant for several consecutive months. Some items, such as department stores, will vary from month to month. For this type of item, enter the amount due in the budget form as soon as the invoice is received. For closer control, accumulate all charge account sales slips and receipts and periodically, perhaps weekly, add them up and compare the total to the variable expense budget. Move these receipts to other files after including them in the total of each variable expense.

Variable expense budgeting could also be named controllable expense budgeting since these types of expenditures are largely discretionary and represent the key to controlling household expenditures. Periodically these expenditures should be evaluated to determine if an excessive amount is being charged to credit accounts, if too little is being allocated to savings, if there is an inadequate amount being allocated to unassigned reserves, etc. Variable expense planning and control are basic requirements for attaining financial success and peace of mind. Knowing the complete financial status all the time, and with only a little effort, makes this budgeting system well worth while. It works well whether there are eight expense items or eighteen.

6. Unassigned Reserve

This item represents the balance of spendable income remaining after all cash, recurring, and variable expense amounts have been budgeted. It is useful for expenditure planning purposes and, of course, as a reserve.

7. Estimated Income Budgeting

On the budget form, enter the monthly income as estimated in the Example 3-5 Estimated Income form. Include those amounts that will actually be received and that will be spendable.

8. Ledger of Actual Expense Payments

The expense items included in the Budget of Cash, Expenses, and Income form should be listed in the same order in this ledger form as shown in Example 3-2. At the time each item is paid, enter the amount and date paid in this ledger.

This ledger provides a summary of all significant household expenditures and, at the same time, serves as the basis for future budgets. It is much easier, it requires less time, and it is more accurate to prepare and maintain this ledger for budget purposes than it is to search through page after page of check book registers for each budget item. It also shows at a glance the budget items that have been paid and those remaining to be paid. Any missing invoices are readily discovered by periodically reviewing this ledger.

The information accumulated in this ledger is useful in determining trends in expenditures, in the planning and controlling of household expenses, and in the preparation of income tax returns.

A separate ledger form, as shown in Example 3-3, should be used to record the amount and date paid for each item of medical, dental, and miscellaneous expense. Payments to doctors, dentists, pharmacies, services organizations, charities, magazines, etc. should be recorded in this ledger for the same reasons as those stated above.

9.   Budget Concept Advantages

The budget concept described above, with a minimum amount of time and effort, provides enough information to plan the use of spendable income, to avoid payment surprises, and to determine the household financial position at any given time. It also provides some flexibility in the payment of expenses. If several significant expense items, such as auto insurance, property taxes, water district charges, and Christmas, all fall within one month, plans for the payment of these expenses may be made several months ahead of payment due dates. In such a situation, it might be prudent to pay some of these expenses a month early or perhaps change the payment due date, such as for auto insurance, to another month. A big advantage in planning is realized by being able to look at budget expenses for a period of several months in advance of payment due dates.

10.   Procedures for Use of Cash and for Payment of Expenses

   A. Deposit all income received in a bank checking account.
   B. On the first of each month, withdraw the budgeted amount of cash for the first half of the month. For closer control of cash expenditures, it is helpful to set aside cash for the period of the first through the seventh and, separately, cash for the period of the eighth through the fifteenth of each month. The same allocation may be made for each week of the second half of each month. For each semi-monthly withdrawal, <u>check off the related amount shown in the household budget</u>.
   C. On the sixteenth of each month, withdraw the budgeted amount of cash for the second half of the month.
   D. Use cash for those expenses not included in the recurring and variable expense budgets. Use cash for food, gasoline, restaurants, cleaners, low-value sundries, and other low-value purchases. This procedure eliminates the need to write many checks or to make many credit and debit card transactions for low-value purchases. Since it provides little or no control of cash expenditures, do not use ATMs to obtain cash.
   E. For most expenses, pay bills twice a month. Sometime between the first and the fourth of each month, pay all bills due by the middle of the month. Between the fifteenth and nineteenth of each month, pay all bills due by the first of the next month. Sometimes, especially for department stores, the payment due date does not permit the twice-a-month payment schedule. In these few cases, of course, pay the bills in a timely manner to avoid late payment charges.
   F. At the time each item is paid, it is important to make a check mark(ü) next to each item listed in the household budget form. This is important because it shows at a glance the paid and unpaid budget items, and it permits an evaluation of the financial position easily and at any time. (see Example 3-4).

National®Brand 45-606 Eye-Ease®
45-306 2 - Pack
Made in USA

NAME: Jim and Sue   YEAR: 2004

	Initials	Date
Prepared By		
Approved By		

BUDGET OF CASH, EXPENSES, AND INCOME

Prepared November, 2003   Example 3-1

Six month budget with bills paid through February

	BUDGET ITEM	(✓) JAN	(✓) FEB	(✓) MAR	(✓) APR	(✓) MAY	(✓) JUNE	
1	1. Cash - 1st Half	$300	$300	$300	$300	$300	$300	1
2	Cash - 2nd Half	300	300	300	300	300	300	2
3	2. Recurring Expenses:							3
4	Church, F.O.P.	260	260	260	260	260	260	4
5	U.S. Bank, mortgage	670	670	670	670	670	670	5
6	AT&T, phone & cable	90	90	90	90	90	90	6
7	PG&E, gas	70	70	70	70	70	70	7
8	So. Cal. Ed., electr	80	80	80	80	80	80	8
9	Smith, yard care	100	100	100	100	100	100	9
10	Insurance	150	150	150	150	150	150	10
11	County sewer & refuse	40	40	40	40	40	40	11
12	Contingency	100	100	100	100	100	100	12
13	AIG Insur., auto (3)	--	--	640	--	--	--	13
14	AIG Insur., home (3)	--	--	520	--	--	--	14
15	Income Tax, est'd(1,4,6)	300	--	--	300	--	300	15
16	Tax returns (4)	--	--	--	150	--	--	16
17	Property taxes (4)	--	--	--	500	--	--	17
18	F.D. Water Dist. (6)	--	--	--	--	--	190	18
19	Registration, auto(5)	--	--	--	--	130	--	19
20								20
21								21
22								22
23	3. Total, Items 1 & 2	2460	2160	3320	3110	2290	2650	23
24	4. Item 6 minus Item 3*	1940	2240	1080	1290	2110	1750	24
25								25
26	5. Variable Expenses:							26
27	College fund	100	100	100	100	200	200	27
28	Line of credit	200	300	200	200	300	100	28
29	Visa	300	700					29
30	Sears	600	200					30
31	Saving/Investment	440	640					31
32								32
33								33
34	Unassigned Reserve	300	300					34
35								35
36	6. Spendable Income	4400	4400	4400	4400	4400	4400	36
37								37
38	Notes: For all items, check-off (✓) when paid.							38
39	For periodic budget items, enter months due-example (1,4,6).							39
40	* Monthly amount available for variable expenses.							40

HOME SWEET WELL MANAGED HOME

		Initials	Date
NAME: Jim and Sue	YEAR: 2004	Prepared By	
BUDGET OF CASH, EXPENSES, AND INCOME		Approved By	

Prepared May, 2004   Example 3-1

	BUDGET ITEM	(✓) JULY	(✓) AUG	(✓) SEPT	(✓) OCT	(✓) NOV	(✓) DEC	
1	1. Cash – 1st – Half	$300	$300	$300	$300	$300	$300	1
2	Cash – 2nd – Half	300	300	300	300	300	300	2
3	2. Recurring Expenses:							3
4	Church, F.O.P.	260	260	260	260	260	260	4
5	U.S. Bank, mortgage	670	670	670	670	670	670	5
6	AT&T, phone & cable	90	90	90	90	90	90	6
7	PG&E, gas	70	70	70	70	70	70	7
8	So.Ca.Ed. electricity	80	80	80	80	80	80	8
9	Smith, yard care	100	100	100	100	100	100	9
10	Insurance	150	150	150	150	150	150	10
11	County sewer & refuse	40	40	40	40	40	40	11
12	Contingency	100	100	100	100	100	100	12
13	AIG Insur., auto (9)	--	--	650	--	--	--	13
14	Income tax, est'd (9)	--	--	300	--	--	--	14
15	Property taxes (11)	--	--	--	--	500	--	15
16	F.O. Water Dist. (12)	--	--	--	--	--	190	16
17	P.B.S. TV (11)	--	--	--	--	120	--	17
18								18
19								19
20								20
21								21
22								22
23	3. Total, Items 1 & 2	2160	2160	3110	2160	2780	2350	23
24	4. Item 6 minus Item 3*	2240	2240	1290	2240	1620	2050	24
25								25
26	5. Variable Expenses							26
27	College fund	200	200	100	200	100	100	27
28	Line of credit	200	100	--	--	--	--	28
29	Visa							29
30	Sears							30
31	Saving/Investment							31
32								32
33								33
34	Unassigned Reserve							34
35								35
36	6. Spendable Income	4400	4400	4400	4400	4400	4400	36
37								37
38	Notes: For all items, check-off (✓) when paid.							38
39	For periodic budget items, enter month due – example (7,9,11)							39
40	* Monthly amount available for variable expenses.							40

National® Brand 45-606 Eye-Ease®
45-306 2 - Pack
Made in USA **NAME: Jim and Sue**   **YEAR: 2004**   Prepared By   Approved By

ACTUAL EXPENSE PAYMENTS - RECURRING AND VARIABLE

Bills Paid through February   Example 3-2

PAYEE (MONTH DUE)	JAN	(*)	FEB	(*)	MAR	(*)	APR	(*)	MAY	(*)	JUNE	(*)
					AMOUNT AND DATE PAID							
Recurring Expenses:												
Church, F.O.P.	260	(1)	260	(1)								
U.S. Bank, mortgage	670	(16)	670	(16)								
AT&T, phone & cable	78	(16)	89	(16)								
PG&E, gas	67	(1)	67	(1)								
So.Ca.Ed., electricity	83	(1)	83	(1)								
Smith, yard care	100	(1)	100	(1)								
Insurance	142	(16)	142	(16)								
County sewer & refuse	38	(1)	38	(1)								
AIG Insur., auto (3)												
AIG Insur., home (3)												
Income tax, est'd(1,4,6)	300	(1)										
Tax returns (4)												
Property taxes (4)												
F.Q. Water Dist. (6)												
Registration, auto(5)												
Variable Expenses:												
College fund	100	(1)	100	(1)								
Line of credit	200	(16)	300	(16)								
Visa	291	(1)	690	(1)								
Sears	592	(16)	187	(16)								
Saving/Investment	450	(1)	640	(1)								

* (Date paid)

National®Brand 45-606 Eye-Ease®
45-306 2 - Pack
Made in USA

	Initials	Date
Prepared By		
Approved By		

NAME: Jim and Sue **YEAR:** 2004

ACTUAL EXPENSE PAYMENTS – RECURRING AND VARIABLE

Example 3-2

	PAYEE (MONTH DUE)	AMOUNT AND DATE PAID					
		JULY (*)	AUG (*)	SEPT (*)	OCT (*)	NOV (*)	DEC (*)
1	Recurring Expenses:						
2	Church, F.O.P.						
3	U.S. Bank, mortgage						
4	AT&T, phone & cable						
5	PG&E, gas						
6	So.Ca.Ed., electricity						
7	Smith, yard work						
8	Insurance						
9	County sewer & refuse						
10	AIG Insur., auto (9)						
11	Income tax, est'd (9)						
12	Property taxes (11)						
13	F.O. Water Dist. (12)						
14	P.B.S. TV (11)						
15							
16							
17							
18							
19							
20							
21							
22							
23							
24							
25							
26	Variable Expenses:						
27	College fund						
28	Visa						
29	Sears						
30	Saving/Investment						
31							
32							
33							
34							
35							
36							
37							
38							
39	* (Date paid)						
40							

HOME SWEET WELL MANAGED HOME

NAME: Jim and Sue   **YEAR:** 2004   Prepared By   Initials   Date

ACTUAL EXPENSE PAYMENTS - MEDICAL, DENTAL, AND MISCELLANEOUS   Approved By

Bills Paid through February   Example 3-3

	DATE	PAYEE	MEDICAL	DENTAL	MISC.	NOTES	
			AMOUNT PAID				
1	1-12	Dr. Morgan		$90		Cleaning & x-ray (Jim)	1
2	1-16	Reader's Digest			$25	12 issues, thru Mar 2005	2
3	1-22	Dr. Simpson	$50			Office visit - cold (Jim)	3
4	1-25	Red Cross			50	Donation	4
5	2-4	Dr. Hayden	75			Eye exam (Sue)	5
6	2-9	Rotary			125	Dues, one year (Jim)	6
7	2-12	United Way			50	Donation	7
8	2-22	Rite Aide Drug	42			Prescription, Zilex (Sue)	8
9	2-28	Golf Digest			28	12 issues, thru April 2005	9

22

National®Brand 45-606 Eye-Ease®
45-306 2 - Pack
Made in USA NAME: Jim and Sue   YEAR: 2004

		Initials	Date
Prepared By			
Approved By			

CALCULATION OF HOUSEHOLD FINANCIAL POSITION

Example 3-4

			AMOUNT
A.	SHORT TERM POSITION		
	TODAYS DATE: October 12, 2004	POSITION DATE: October 31, 2004	
	1. Cash on hand today		$220
	2. Add checking account balance today (from register)		480
	3. Add income expected from today through position date		2,250
	4. Total amount available — sum of Items 1, 2, and 3		$2,950
	For the period from today through the position date:		
	5. Subtract unpaid recurring expense budget items		(800)
	6. Subtract unpaid estimated variable expenses		(900)
	7. Subtract other known planned expenditures		(700)
	8. Total of subtracted Items 5, 6, and 7		$2,400
	9. Unassigned net amount on position date (Item 4 less Item 8)		$550
B.	LONG TERM POSITION (USE WHOLE MONTH AMOUNTS ONLY)		AMOUNT
	(Based on Example 3-1 Budget)		
	Evaluation Period (start and end months): Jan. thru June 2004		
	1. Total spendable income		$26,400
	2. Total budgeted cash and recurring expenses		15,990
	3. Total available for variable (controllable) expenses*		$10,410
	* College funds, savings, credit purchases, reserves, or other discretionary expenditures.		

National®Brand 45-606 Eye-Ease®
45-306 2 - Pack
Made in USA

NAME: Jim and Sue   **YEAR:** 2004   Prepared By

ESTIMATED SPENDABLE INCOME   Approved By

Example 3-5

	SOURCE OF INCOME	JAN	FEB	MAR	APR	MAY	JUNE	
1								1
2	Salary/Wages:							2
3	First	$3900	$3900	$3900	$3900	$3900	$3900	3
4	Second							4
5	Commissions							5
6	Bonus							6
7	Company Pension:							7
8	First							8
9	Second							9
10	Social Security:							10
11	First							11
12	Second							12
13	401 K Proceeds:							13
14	First							14
15	Second							15
16	Interest (Bonds,Banks,etc)	500	500	500	500	500	500	16
17	Dividends (Stocks,Funds)							17
18	Rentals							18
19	Trust Proceeds							19
20	Other:							20
21	First							21
22	Second							22
23	Third							23
24	Fourth							24
25								25
26								26
27								27
28								28
29								29
30								30
31	TOTAL:	$4400	$4400	$4400	$4400	$4400	$4400	31
32								32
33								33
34								34
35								35
36	Note: Enter monthly totals in the Income section of the Budget of							36
37	Cash, Expenses, and Income form.							37
38								38
39								39
40								40

		Initials	Date
NAME: Jim and Sue	YEAR: 2004	Prepared By	
ESTIMATED SPENDABLE INCOME		Approved By	

Example 3-5

	1	2	3	4	5	6
SOURCE OF INCOME	JULY	AUG	SEPT	OCT	NOV	DEC
Salary/Wages:						
First	$3900	$3900	$3900	$3900	$3900	$3900
Second						
Commissions						
Bonus						
Company Pension:						
First						
Second						
Social Security:						
First						
Second						
401 K Proceeds:						
First						
Second						
Interest (Bonds,Bank,etc)						
Dividends (Stocks,Funds)						
Rentals	500	500	500	500	500	500
Trust Proceeds						
Other:						
First						
Second						
Third						
Fourth						
TOTAL:	$4400	$4400	$4400	$4400	$4400	$4400

Note: Enter monthly totals in the Income section of the Budget of
Cash, Expenses, and Income form.

CHAPTER 4

ESSENTIAL HOUSEHOLD FILES

BUDGETS AND LEDGERS
LEGAL DOCUMENTS
INSURANCE
INVESTMENT ASSETS
INCOME TAX RETURNS
PERSONAL PROPERTY ASSETS
SOCIAL SECURITY
EDUCATION PLANS
CHARGE ACCOUNT INVOICES

ESSENTIAL HOUSEHOLD FILES

There are two broad categories of files:

1. Active
2. Closed

ACTIVE FILES

All active files should be stored in a fire proof, lockable file cabinet. Start with a two-drawer cabinet with a fire resistance rating of at least 1700 degrees for one hour. The importance of this type of file cabinet cannot be overstated. The most efficient location for it is adjacent to the desk or table at which the household business is conducted. The contents of this cabinet, filed in hanging files with manila folders, should include at least the following documents and at least one folder for each numbered item and for each listed document.

1. **Budgets and Ledgers**

   A. Current budget of cash, expenses, and income; current ledger of actual expense payments, recurring and variable; current ledger of actual expense payments - medical, dental, and miscellaneous; current estimated income forms; and calculations of current household financial positions.
   B. Completed and closed documents of above Item A. Since these are a good reference source for the preparation of future budgets, file these documents in the active file for a period of three years.

2. **Legal Documents**

   A. Copy of the valid living trust or will. The signed and notarized original should be stored in a bank safety deposit box.
   B. Copy of living trust (or will) extracts, amendments, codicils, and all trust funding documents.
   C. Records of gifting and loans made to trust (or will) beneficiaries – one folder for each beneficiary. Record of each gift and unpaid loan balance by calendar year.

D. All house purchase documents – inspection reports, financing data and notes, title report, purchase agreement, closing statement, and a copy of recorded trust deeds. The original trust deed documents should be stored in a bank safety deposit box.

3.   Insurance

A. Ordinary life insurance policies, amendments, letters, and invoices.
B. Irrevocable life insurance trust policies, letters, annual statements, and loan documents.
C. Auto insurance policies, amendments, letters, and invoices.
D. House insurance policies, amendments, letters, and invoices.
E. Umbrella and other policies, amendments, letters, and invoices.
F. Insurance claim documents – one folder for each claim.

4.   Investment Asset

A. Master investment record.
B. Copy of each stock certificate, transaction record, and dividend check stub received. The original certificates should be stored in a bank safety deposit box.
C. Copy of each bond certificate, transaction record, and interest check stub received. The original certificates should be stored in a bank safety deposit box.
D. Use one folder for the documents pertaining to each savings account and to other certificates and notes acquired.
E. For each mutual fund investment, a copy of the application, purchase confirmation record, and periodic reports.
F. Each promissory note for money owed to you, and the record of note repayments.
G. Each promissory note for money you owe to others and the record of note repayments.

5.   Income Tax Returns

A. For each year, basic data needed to prepare federal and state income tax returns including reports of interest and dividends earned, W-2's, 1098's, 1099's, pension reports, date and price of each investment bought and sold, average cost summaries, contribution receipts, interest paid, etc.
B. For each year, copies of completed and signed federal and state income tax returns.

6.   Personal Property Assets

Use one file folder for each item of personal property purchased. Include a folder for each low-priced, medium-priced, and high-priced item. Exclude household supplies and personal property items filed in other sections of the file cabinet. The tab of each folder should include the name of the item and date purchased. For example, "Refrigerator, Kenmore, Purchased October 17, 2002."

For each item, include the sales receipt, purchase contract, operating instructions, warranty notice, installation instructions, assembly instructions, parts lists, deeds of trust, etc. A hundred or more folders might be required for this file section. File these folders in alphabetical order using the item names found on the folder tabs.

7.   Social Security

A.   Original Social Security cards, annual notices of your new benefit amount, direct deposit sign up forms, applications for Social Security benefits and approval/award letters, annual report of earnings, and benefit information letters and booklets.

B.   Original Social Security Act Health Insurance cards, notices of medical insurance enrollment and premium deductions, and benefit information letter and booklets.

8.   Education Plans

A.   Description of education plans and blank semester planning work forms.

B.   Use one file folder for each child for whom an education fund has been established. Include in each folder a master record of investments, investment withdrawals and payments to students, investment reports, date and price of each investment bought and sold, average cost summaries, and completed student semester planning work forms.

9.   Charge Account Invoices

All invoices/sales receipts received for each charge account purchase. For this file, use a shoebox-size box. Keep each invoice/sales receipt for perhaps a year, and then shred and discard it.

CLOSED FILES

Closed files should be stored in a lockable file cabinet located near the desk or table at which household business is conducted. The contents of this cabinet, filed in manila folders (hanging files are unnecessary), should include at least the following documents – usually transferred from the active files:

1.   Completely superseded copies of living trusts, wills, amendments, codicils, and trust funding documents.

2.   After the sale of a dwelling, all original purchase documents.

3.   A copy of each investment asset document after each sale or redemption of stocks, bonds, annuities, mutual funds, etc.

4.   A copy of each paid-in-full promissory note.

5.   Copies of all completed and submitted federal and state income tax returns and all supporting documentation.

6.   Social Security documents, such as annual benefit notices, pertaining to previous years.

Retain these documents for at least eight years, and then shred and discard them.
The following documents should be shredded and discarded:

1. Household budgets and ledgers older than three years.
2. Life, auto, and umbrella insurance documents that have been superseded by up-to-date policies. Insurance claim documents older than eight years.
3. Each file folder document pertaining to personal property assets that have been replaced or discarded.
4. Education plans and related documents that are outdated or are inactive because the education fund has been depleted.
5. Charge account invoices and sales receipts older than one year.

It is easier by far to set up and maintain well organized files than it is to periodically search through stacks of unsorted documents.

CHAPTER 5

ESSENTIALS OF HOUSEHOLD INSURANCE

TERM LIFE INSURANCE
WHOLE LIFE INSURANCE
UNIVERSAL LIFE INSURANCE
SURVIVORSHIP LIFE INSURANCE
HOME OWNERS INSURANCE
AUTO INSURANCE
UMBRELLA INSURANCE
REAL PROPERTY TITLE INSURANCE

ESSENTIALS OF HOUSEHOLD INSURANCE

Start with a careful evaluation of your insurance protection needs. Before the first insurance purchase and periodically thereafter you should obtain the help of a certified financial advisor who is not an insurance agent. The objective is to acquire adequate protection without becoming "insurance poor."

After this insurance protection evaluation is made, obtain insurance quotes from several reputable companies or by using a computer and then, from the lowest bidder, purchase policies that best cover your exposure to loss.

There are several basic types of insurance coverages that should be considered:

1. Life insurance
2. Home owners insurance
3. Auto insurance
4. Personal liability umbrella insurance
5. Real property title insurance

1.   Life Insurance

Term insurance covers a person against death for a limited time, the term. Each year, a premium is paid for insurance protection for that year. The term, for example, might be one that lasts until children are married or until retirement. The only way to collect from a term policy is to die during the term. Many companies offer level-premium term insurance wherein the premiums remain the same for a period of perhaps five up to thirty years. Some companies guarantee the level premiums and some do not. It is preferable to obtain a guaranteed premium policy. This is one reason for you to understand the terms of any policy you are considering. At the end of the term, the contract or policy expires with no residual value. Under a mortgage protection term insurance policy the face amount decreases over time, consistent with the projected annual decreases in the outstanding balance of a mortgage loan. Mortgage protection policies usually cover a range of mortgage repayment periods such as 15, 20, 25, or 30 years. Although the death benefit decreases, the premium is usually level in amount. Further, the premium payment period often is shorter than the maximum period of insurance coverage – for example, a twenty-year mortgage protection policy might require that premiums be paid over the first seventeen years.

Whole life insurance is one designed to remain in effect throughout one's lifetime. If you continue to pay the premiums it does not expire. It is well suited to objectives that remain constant over a long period of time such as paying estate settlement costs and taxes. This type of policy provides coverage similar to that of term life insurance. These policies develop cash values which may be accessed by the owner through cash surrenders or policy loans. The value of the policy, over time, may be enhanced by two components: a guaranteed cash value which typically grows based on a pre-determined schedule and, secondly, by a non-guaranteed cash value element made up of dividends or excess interest.

Universal life insurance is another permanent type of coverage that itemizes the protection element, the expense element, and the cash value element. With this separation more flexibility may be built into the policy and, within certain restrictions, allows the policy owner to modify the face amount or the premiums in response to changing needs and circumstances. Each month, interest is credited to the policy based upon the cash value of the policy and based on the current declared interest rate as determined by the insurance company. Also, each month, certain amounts are deducted to cover the cost of the death benefits and the costs of any riders or supplemental benefits. Additionally, there is a surrender value based on the cash value less any applicable surrender charge. This type of policy may be used in an irrevocable insurance trust for the purpose of eventually paying for a specific objective such as estate taxes.

Survivorship or second-to-die life insurance coverage, typically whole life or universal life, pays a death benefit at the later death of two insured individuals, usually a husband and wife. It is a method of discounting any future estate tax liabilities. These second-to-die contracts allow the insurance company to delay payment of the death benefit until the second insured's death, thereby providing benefits with which to pay taxes exactly when they are needed. This coverage is generally less expensive than individual insurance coverage.

Life insurance choices need to be established on a case-by-case basis. It is painful to pay for life insurance but only a few can do without it. Buy adequate life insurance but remember that people with no dependents may not need life policies at all. It is important to buy life insurance only for those losses, such as your income, that you or your family cannot replace. Avoid narrowly defined policies that only cover specific loss of life such as accidents, plane crashes, or cancer. You're better off with insurance for any loss of life for a small increase in premiums.

To estimate the amount of a life insurance policy, estimate your dependents basic living expenses if your income is no longer available. The recommended policy amount is one that is six to eight times your annual income.

Term life insurance policies best fit the needs of young families with large financial obligations. The relatively lower premiums enable them to purchase sufficient coverage to protect against loss of income. Any discretionary investment funds can be placed in other vehicles for a better return—places such as mutual funds, certificates of deposit, stocks, bonds, etc. Cash value insurance, whole and universal, is sometimes purchased to pay for estate settlement costs and taxes.

2.   Home Owners Insurance

The basic essential coverages are dwelling, other structures, personal property, loss of use, personal liability, and medical payments to others. By all means select and pay for replacement – "new for old" coverage for your dwelling and personal property. Many options are available including insurance for floods, earthquakes, molds/fungi, jewelry and furs (valued at more than the basic coverage), personal computers and electronics, antiques, silverware, fine arts, special collections, golf carts, added property and liability needs, building code upgrades, etc.

Some insurers offer discounts for such items as monitored burglar alarm systems, both home and auto policies, and a claim free record. See Example 5-1, Homeowners Policy Declarations, for a typical statement of coverages, limits, loss settlement provisions, forms, options, endorsements, deductibles, annual premium, list of premium reductions, and effective dates.

3. Auto Insurance

The basic essential coverages are liability/bodily injury, property damage, medical payments, comprehensive, collision, uninsured motor vehicle, property damage, and uninsured motor vehicle bodily injury. Liability provides coverage when there is damage to others. Medical payments are for medical and funeral expenses. Comprehensive covers your car when it is damaged – except by collision or upset. Collision covers your car when it is damaged by collision or upset. Uninsured motor vehicle property damage applies when the other car or driver is not insured and there is property damage. Uninsured motor vehicle is coverage when the other car or driver is not insured or is underinsured and there is bodily injury to an insured.

There are a number of options available including emergency road service, car rental expense, car rental and travel expenses, loss of earnings, total disability, coverage for death, dismemberment, and loss of sight, etc.

Premium reductions are sometimes offered for driving safety/good driver record, length of time with the same insurer, vehicle safety (air bags, anti-lock brakes, type of auto), both auto or two or more autos, and home policies with the same insurance company, driving defense course etc.

Other elements may affect the amount of your premium including drivers of your car and their ages and marital status, your car type and its use, eligibility for premium credits, and applicability of surcharge based either on accident history or on other factors. See Example 5-2, Automobile Policy Declarations, for a typical statement of coverages, limits, description of auto including identification number, age of primary driver, average miles auto driven per year, premium, list of premium reductions, and effective dates.

The amount of deductibles for home owners, collision, and comprehensive policies should be determined as part of the original and periodic evaluations recommended at the beginning of this chapter.

4. Personal Liability Umbrella Insurance

This type of insurance provides for personal liability coverage in a specified amount over and above the liability insurance set forth in the underlying automobile policy. If your bodily injury limit is $500,000 in your automobile policy and $1,000,000 in your umbrella policy, then your total liability coverage limit would be $1,500,000. To be applicable, the underlying automobile insurance policy must be paid and in force and must be continued in force for as long as you wish to continue your umbrella coverage. See Example 5-3, Umbrella Policy Declarations, for a typical statement of coverages, limits, forms, endorsements, underlying automobile exposures, annual premiums, and effective dates.

It is important to recognize that if you are legally obligated to pay damages for a loss, you are personally responsible for the payment of those damages that exceed your personal liability insurance coverage. These overage payments could be financially disastrous and could involve legal attachment (garnishee) on your property and income.

Typically, your insurance company representatives will investigate, negotiate, and settle a claim or suit covered by your umbrella policy. Costs usually paid by your insurer include legal defense of your suit, premiums on any bonds that are required, expenses incurred by you or by the insurer's representatives including any actual loss of your earnings, prejudgment interest awarded against you, and, of course, the awarded judgment amount. All obligations of the insurance company end when payments for claim defense and damages equals the limit of the liability stated in your policies.

In your policies there are many exclusions from the coverages your insurance company will pay. To know about and understand these exclusions are as important, if not more so, than knowing what the policies do cover.

5. Real Property Title Insurance

When you buy any real estate it is essential that you purchase owners title insurance. Imagine buying a home and then discovering after you move in that the deeds were forged and that the person who sold you the property didn't own it. This can and does happen. Some states require that all property buyers purchase owners title insurance, and other states don't. If you live in a state that doesn't require it, and you don't get it, you have set yourself up for a financial catastrophe. Even if you buy from a relative or from your best friend, be certain to purchase title insurance.

Owners title insurance protects you against such problems as the sellers not owning the property, forged powers of attorney, easement problems, law suits filed by heirs to property that was sold illegally, mortgage loans on property that buyers weren't told about, hidden liens, and other problems.

For this type of insurance a one-time payment only is made for a policy that protects your equity in the property for as long as you or your heirs own it.

It is essential that you obtain and pay for insurance protection but only the kinds and amounts that you really need

It should be recognized that if you faithfully prepare and maintain an asset file as described in Chapter Four, you do not need to keep a separate inventory of personal property. However, photographs of special collections and other high-value items could be of some value. Such photographs should be stored in the household asset file.

Example 5-1

Homeowners Policy Declarations

1. Coverages and Limits

Dwelling	$237,400
Dwelling Extension	23,740
Personal Property	178,050
Loss of Use	Actual Loss
Personal Liability	100,000
Damage to Property of Others	500
Medical Payments to Others, Per Person	5,000

2. **Loss Settlement Provision**

Replacement Cost for Similar Construction

Replacement Cost Limit – 120% of basic coverage

3. **Deductibles**

All Losses	1,000

4. **Option Coverage**

Jewelry and Furs	2,500/5,000
Increase for Loss of Dwelling	47,480
County Ordinance Upgrades	23,740

5. **Premium Reductions**

Home Alert System – 10%

Claim Free Record – 10%

Home and Auto Insured – 5%

6. Net Annual Premium $808

Example 5-2

Auto Policy Declarations

1. **Coverage and Limits**
   Liability:
   Bodily Injury, Each Person/Total $250,000/500,000
   Property Damage 100,000
   Medical Payments 10,000
   Uninsured Motor Vehicle:
   Bodily Injury, Each Person/Total 100,000/300,000

2. **Deductibles**
   Comprehensive 250
   Collision 500

3. **Basis of Premium**
   2002 Toyota Camry   VIN xxxxx
   Driven 7,500 miles or less annually
   Principal driver has 48 years of driving experience.
   Pleasure use or driving to and from work.

4. **Premium Reductions**
   Multiple Line – House and Auto Insured
   Vehicle Safety
   Driving Safety Record
   California Good Driver
   Years with Insurer

5. **Net Semi-Annual Premium** $547

Example 5-3

Umbrella Policy Declarations

1. **Coverages and Limits**
    Personal Liability $1,000,000

2. **Automobile Exposures**
    Automobile Liability   One Auto
    Automobile Operators   One

3. **Net Annual Premium** $149

CHAPTER 6

ESSENTIALS OF LIVING TRUSTS AND WILLS

LIVING TRUST
POWER OF ATTORNEY FOR ASSET MANAGEMENT
POWER OF ATTORNEY FOR HEALTH CARE DECISIONS

ESSENTIALS OF LIVING TRUSTS AND WILLS

Living trusts and wills are legal documents that include instructions for where you want you're property to go after you die. Also included are assignments of trustees, conservators, executors, administrators, power of attorney for asset management, power of attorney for health care decisions, and instructions for final medical treatment desires and limitations. These documents are an essential part of estate planning. Without them you are, in effect, leaving it to state law to dictate how your property will be distributed.

There are several types of estate planning techniques available to you including a basic revocable living trust, a basic will, a bypass trust, a qualified terminable interest property trust, and a marital deduction trust. For most people the first two techniques – a basic living trust and basic will – will be all that is necessary. Only these two are addressed in this chapter. There can be a living trust specifically for married couples or there can be a single person trust.

Estate planning, at least the use of living trusts and wills, is not just for elderly or wealthy people. Many young and middle age people die suddenly, often leaving minor children behind who need care. If you own only modest assets, you should dictate how they are to be distributed when you die.

Your revocable living trust must be funded and then managed. Funding of a trust requires that the title of all your significant assets be changed from you to your trust. This includes title to all real property, bank accounts, stock and bond certificates, mutual fund holdings, and other investments, automobiles, etc. These title transfers simply mean that your trust owns the assets and you, as trustee, own the trust. For transferring real property to your trust a "quit claim deed" may be used. This deed is to be recorded in your county recording office or other local government entity. Personal property such as bank accounts, stocks and bonds, automobiles, etc., can be transferred by contacting the bank or office where the asset is recorded or held.

As trustee you are responsible for managing the trust assets just as you did before the trust was established. You should always keep careful records of all transactions that effect your revocable living trust; however, there is no need for special accounting records or tax return forms. Title of new assets acquired should be assigned to your trust at the time of acquisition.

When you place assets in your trust, you should identify the title of those assets as belonging to "(your name) Trustee of the (your name) Family Trust, established (date established)."

Periodically perhaps every five years, your trust should be reviewed and updated. Any changes or additions may be made by the use of written, signed and notarized amendments (sequentially numbered).

For estates with a total value that is less than the federal estate tax deductible amount and which includes straight-forward distribution instructions a paralegal company may be used for the preparation of a living trust. For estates of higher value or for those with extensive distribution instructions, the living trust should be prepared by an attorney specializing in this type of work.

Basic Essentials of a Living Trust – A Layman's Explanation

1. A declaration page including the official name of the trust and statements that the trust was made and executed in the United States of America and that it shall be governed by the laws of America.

2. A summary of your revocable living trust in which you provide a general description of the provisions to ensure that your wishes are carried out.

3. Transfer In Trust Article - This article states that the person establishing the Trust (the Trustor or Grantor) has transferred various assets (the Trust Estate) to the Trustees of the Trust and identifies such assets according to the Trust provisions, to eventually distribute the assets to those persons named as beneficiaries.

4. Disposition During The Life of The Trustor Article – This article requires the Trustees to pay as much of the income and principal of the Trust assets to the Trustor as might be requested. Briefly, the Trustor, before death, may use or spend the Trust assets as freely as he/she did before the asset was transferred to the Trust. All income is considered paid out to the trustor.

5. Disposition on Death of The Trustor Article – This Article distributes the Trust assets, at the death of the Trustor, to the family or heirs. Various paragraphs may include directions to the Trustees to provide for the education and support of minor or incapable children, grandchildren, or other beneficiaries, specific bequests of personal effects or assets, or distributions to charity. Distributions may be equal or unequal, measured in exact dollars or percentages of the estate, giving in lumps sums or in periodic, fractional payments. Directions to the Trustees can be precise and mandatory, or discretionary with the Trustees in the manner of their execution. This section really is the "heart" of the estate plan, and is drafted to satisfy the Trustor's unique planning desires. The Article also directs the Trustees to distribute the Trustor's personal effects according to certain letter(s) of instruction written by the Trustor.

6. Spendthrift Provision Article – This "spendthrift" paragraph prevents a child or other beneficiary, other than the Trustor, from pledging, mortgaging, assigning away, or otherwise using any expected inheritance from the Trust to satisfy, or serve as collateral for a loan or other indebtedness.

7. Invalid Provisions Article – This article directs that if some provision of the Trust is ever held invalid, because of legal contest or change in the law, the other unaffected provisions, if possible, are to be carried out by the Trustees consistent with the overall purposes of the Trust.

8. Perpetuities Savings Clause – It is against public policy for a Trust to continue for unreasonable lengths of time, such as for hundreds of years. To comply with an Old English law still in effect known as the "Rule Against Perpetuities", this clause requires the Trust to terminate no later than twenty-one years after the death of the survivor of the Trustor and their issue (including children, grandchildren, great-grandchildren, etc.) who were living on the date the Trust was executed.

9. Trustees Article – The Trustees, or managers, of the Trust assets are named in this paragraph, and serve in the order listed. Generally, the Trustor will be the initial Trustee. At the death of the Trustor, the Trustee named in paragraph "Second" or "Third" will hold or distribute the Trust assets to the beneficiaries.

10. Powers of the Trustee Article – The powers of the Trustor (while alive and acting as Trustee) are very broad to allow the Trustor unlimited use of all assets. When the successor Trustee is in place, he too is allowed broad power to manage and distribute the estate in accordance with provisions of the trust.

11. Delegation of Authority Article – In the event that the Trustor becomes mentally or physically unable to conduct his affairs, the next successor Trustee(s) may continue to manage the Trust assets with full power until he/she is capable of resuming Trust affairs. During such period of incapacitation the Trust is unamendable and irrevocable.

12. Additions to Trust Article – The Trustor may add assets to the Trust at anytime by simply taking title to them in the name of the active Trustees. Assets initially acquired in the Trustor's name may be deeded or legally transferred from the Trustor, as an individual, to himself as Trustee. The following format will usually serve for title purposes: **Edna Mae Hall**, trustee(s) of **The Edna Mae Hall Trust**.

13. Parties Dealing With Trustees Article – Freedom is granted to the current Trustee to operate the assets of the Trust. Any agent of securities, stocks or investments is not held responsible for verifying the distribution of such assets. The Trustee shall enjoy the same freedom of transactions that the Trustor had.

14. Revocation and Amendment Article – This Trust is capable of being amended or revoked by the Trustor at anytime during his/her lifetime. The Trustor may add, remove, or dispose of all the assets in the Trust without restriction.

15. Vested Interest of Beneficiaries Article – The beneficiaries of the Trust retain all rights to the assets of the Trust that cannot be denied except in the event the Trustor revokes or amends the Trust.

16. Governing Law Article – The Trust is governed by the laws of the state in which it was created. However, it is capable of holding assets that are considered out-of-state.

17. Catastrophic Illness Article – In the event of catastrophic illness of the Trustor, the successor Trustee will serve until such time as the Trustor is capable of resuming the management of the Trust. A definition of catastrophic illness is given.

18. In Terrorem Article – An "In Terrorem" clause is considered very important to eliminate possible court battles among the heirs. If an heir is not satisfied with his share (usually because he feels he deserves more), the next step is to sue the trust. This is a futile effort, but it certainly causes great divisions among family members, and some family members will never forgive such actions. The "In Terrorem" clause simply says that any contest of the divisions or provisions of this trust will mean the loss of the contester's share.

19. Attorney Representation Article – The attorney of record who was involved in the preparation of the trust is named here. With the assistance of a qualified Estate Planning Attorney, as named in this Article, most Trusts can be settled quickly when one of the Trustors dies. This is especially true if the Trust has been updated frequently to reflect changing assets and estate

planning laws. An Attorney specializing in Estate Planning should be able to work more expediently and completely, and less expensively, than one not familiar with this area of law.

20. Prepared in Duplicate Article – The Trust is signed in duplicate, and one copy is given to the Trustor and one to the attorney. If one copy is lost or destroyed, the other signed copy will still be binding.

21. "Pour Over" Last Will and Testament. This document includes a direction that the entire estate shall be added to, administered, and distributed as part of an in-place, named trust. It could also include instructions regarding payment of taxes and debts and incorporation of trust provisions by reference. Nominations of executor and successive executors, and the powers of those nominations, are included in this type of will.

A basic, simple trust document and "pour over" will for an individual are included herein as Examples 6-1 and 6-2.

Essentials of a Comprehensive Living Trust for a Husband and Wife––List of Articles and Sections.

ARTICLE 1: DECLARATION OF TRUST

 1.01. Establishment of Revocable Living Trust

 1.02. Trust Particulars

 1.03. Property Status – Community and Separate

 1.04. Special "Children" Definition

 1.05. Allocation of Trust Estate

ARTICLE 2: TRUST DURING JOINT LIVES OF SETTLORS

 2.01. Introduction

 2.02. Use of Community Income – Broad Standard

 2.03. Use of Community Principal – Broad Standard

 2.04. Use of Separate Income - Broad Standard

 2.05. Separate Principal - Broad Standard

 2.06. Settlors' Incapacity – Ascertainable Standard

 2.07. Community Payments – Special Duty

 2.08. Guidelines – Other Sources Considered

 2.09. Payments to Others

 2.10. Revocation During Settlors' Lives

 2.11. Amendment During Settlors' Lives

 2.12. Powers of Revocation and Amendment Personal

ARTICLE 3: TRUST ALLOCATION AFTER FIRST SPOUSE'S DEATH

 3.01. Action at First Spouse's Death

 3.02. Simultaneous Death – Presumption of Survival

 3.03. Deceased Spouse's Expenses and Taxes

 3.04. Allocation of Surviving Spouse's Property

Essentials of Power of Attorney Appointments

Appointment of Power of Attorney for Asset Management

1. This appointment is also known as "Springing Durable Power of Attorney" and "Attorney-In-Fact Appointed". This appointment becomes effective with the notarized signing of the assignment document by the principal and continues in effect until the death of the principal or until the appointment is revoked or terminated. This power of attorney assignment will continue for an indefinite period of time unless the duration is limited in the assignment document. Every person who owns assets and is at least eighteen years old should appoint this type of power of attorney.

2. The appointment of a power of attorney should be made only after careful consideration of several factors. Since the person you designate has broad powers to dispose of or otherwise manage your real and personal property, you must be able to completely trust this person. It is most convenient and efficient if this person lives within a short distance from the principal and one that has knowledge of the principal's assets. It is also important for the designated appointee to have some knowledge of living trusts, investments, household finances, and real estate procedures.

3. Asset management by the appointee begins on the incapacity of the principal. This incapacity should be established by written and signed opinions of two (2) licensed physicians that the principal is physically or mentally incapable of managing his/her finances and assets. Proof of authority of the designated power of attorney includes the signed and notarized assignment document and the two (2) opinion letters from physicians. Of course, these letters should be filed with the copy of the assignment document. Third parties may rely on the Attorney-In-Fact's authority without further evidence of incapacity.

4. At any time before the principal becomes incapacitated, this power of attorney may be changed by the principal and, by written notice of either party, may be terminated.

5. The basic essentials of a power of attorney appointment document are set forth in Example 6-3.

6. At physical or mental incapacity, the attorney-in-fact should check the trust documents for specific instructions of the principal. Have each physician write a letter documenting the health conditions of the principal.

    A. Notify the bank and other financial institutions that you now have the power of attorney for this person. The bank representative will probably need to see a copy of the trust document, the physician's letter, and your personal identification. Notify any insurance companies that have a disability waiver, such as life insurance, long term care policies, disability policies, etc. Transact any necessary business for the disabled person according to the trust instructions.

    B. Keep records of any bills and income received.

    C. Make sure you keep all the succeeding trustees informed.

7. Upon the death of the principal, the attorney-in-fact should notify the family of your position and assist as needed. The trust has funeral arrangements that should be followed. Give copies of the trust document to all beneficiaries. Make sure you keep all succeeding trustees informed throughout the process. Order at least 12 certified death certificates which usually can be obtained at the funeral home. You will need these to notify life insurance companies, transfer titles, etc.

Notify the trust company that prepared the trust documents so that it is aware of the death, in case you, the beneficiaries or family members, need to call to have questions answered. Notify the bank so you can start writing checks, etc. The bank will need to see a death certificate, a copy of the trust and your identification. Notify Social Security, retirement plans, associations, life insurance companies, etc. These should be listed in the trust.

Collect any bills and start a ledger of accounts payable and income received. Pay all bills and taxes. Contact an accountant for preparation of final State and Federal income tax returns and estate tax forms. Make a final accounting record of all the assets and bills you have paid. You should have copies made for all the beneficiaries when the property is distributed.

Distribute the property in the order the trust has instructed you to follow. Be sure to get a receipt signed by each beneficiary in the trust. On remaining personal property, hold an estate sale if necessary. Divide cash and transfer title of property according to the trust's instructions.

Appointment of Power of Attorney for Health Care Decisions and Medical Treatment Desires and Limitations

1. As with the power of attorney for asset management, you must be able to completely trust this person – even to the point of trusting this person to make life or death decisions for you when you are incapable of doing so.
2. This appointment becomes effective only upon the incapacitation of the principal.
3. The appointed agent and all care givers must follow the terms, conditions, treatment desires, and limitations set forth by the principal in the appointment document.
4. Your doctors will give you information and advice about treatment. You have the right to choose. You can say "Yes" to treatments you want. You can say "No" to any treatment that you don't want – even if the treatment might keep you alive longer. Your doctor must tell you about your medical condition and about what different treatments and pain management alternatives can do for you. Many treatments have "side effects." Your doctor must offer you information about serious problems that medical treatment is likely to cause you. Often, more than one treatment might help you – and people have different ideas about which is best. Your doctor can tell you which treatments are available to you, but your doctor can't choose for you. That choice depends on what is important to you.
5. If you can't make treatment decisions, your doctor will ask your closest available relative or friend to help decide what is best for you. Most of the time that works. But sometimes everyone doesn't agree about what to do. That's why it is helpful if you say in advance what you want to happen if you can't speak for yourself. You can do this through an "advance directive," which you can use to say what you want and who you want to speak for you. One kind of advance directive lets you name someone to make health care decisions when you can't. This form is called a POWER OF ATTORNEY FOR HEALTH CARE DECISIONS. You may fill out this form if you are 18 years or older and of sound mind. You do not need a lawyer to fill it out. You can choose an adult relative or friend you trust as your "agent" to speak for you when you're too sick to make your own decisions. After you choose someone, talk to that person about what you want. You can also write down in the POWER OF ATTORNEY FOR HEALTH CARE DECISIONS when you would or wouldn't want medical treatment. Talk to your doctor about what you want and give your doctor a copy of the form. Give another copy to the person named as your agent.

And take a copy with you when you go into a hospital or other treatment facility. An adequate form for this purpose is shown in Example 6-4.

Sometimes treatment decisions are hard to make and it truly helps your family and your doctors if they know what you want. This POWER OF ATTORNEY also gives them legal protection when they follow your wishes.

6. The POWER OF ATTORNEY FOR HEALTH CARE DECISIONS form has a section which allows you to give specific instructions about your health care without naming an agent. You can also use another kind of advance directive to write down your wishes about treatment. This is often called a "living will" because it takes effect while you are still alive but have become unable to speak for yourself. If you do not wish to appoint a POWER OF ATTORNEY FOR HEALTH CARE DECISIONS, you can just write down your wishes on a piece of paper. Your doctors and family can use what you write in deciding about your treatment. But living wills that don't meet the requirements of the POWER OF ATTORNEY FOR HEALTH CARE don't give as much legal protection for your doctors if a disagreement arises about following your wishes. You can change or revoke your POWER OF ATTORNEY appointment at anytime as long as you can communicate your wishes.

7. You don't have to fill out any of these pre-printed forms if you don't want to. You may choose an adult relative or friend to make decisions for a limited time without filling out a POWER OF ATTORNEY FOR HEALTH CARE DECISIONS form. In this case, you must tell your doctor who you would like to make your decisions and he or she will write it in your medical chart. You can change your mind at any time, but you must notify your doctor so he or she can make the change in your medical chart. If you do not have someone to make decisions for you and do not wish to fill out a POWER OF ATTORNEY FOR HEALTH CARE, you can just talk with your doctors and ask them to write down what you've said in your medical chart. And you can talk with your family. But people will be more clear about your treatment wishes if you write them down. And your wishes are more likely to be followed if you write them down.

8. Regardless of whether or not you appoint someone to decide for you, you will still get medical treatment. You should know that if you become too sick to make decisions someone else will have to make them for you. Remember that:

> A POWER OF ATTORNEY FOR HEALTH CARE DECISIONS lets you name someone to make treatment decisions for you. That person can make most medical decisions – not just those about life sustaining treatment – when you can't speak for yourself.

> If you don't have someone you want to name to make decisions when you can't, you can use the POWER OF ATTORNEY FOR HEALTH CARE form to specify when you would and wouldn't want particular kinds of treatments.

Example 6-1[1]*

**THIS DECLARATION OF TRUST IS
CREATED UNDER ARTICLE 1, SECTION 10 OF THE
CONSTITUTION OF THE UNITED STATES OF AMERICA,
KNOWN AS "THE LAW OF CONTRACT"**

THIS DECLARATION OF TRUST IS MADE AND EXECUTED
IN THE UNITED STATES OF AMERICA
AND SHALL BE CONSTRUED, INTERPRETED AND
GOVERNED BY THE LAWS OF THE UNITED STATES OF AMERICA
AND THE LAWS OF ILLINOIS
As Set Forth in this Declaration of Trust
Its Trustees
Are Authorized to Operate Under the Name of
The Edna Mae Hall Trust

THIS DECLARATION OF TRUST IS REVOCABLE

---

[1] * Pages 6-23 through 6-45

HOME SWEET WELL MANAGED HOME

The Edna Mae Hall Trust

HOME SWEET WELL MANAGED HOME

The Edna Mae Hall Trust

ARTICLE I
Transfer in Trust

For good and valuable consideration, the Trustor, **Edna Mae Hall** of Normal, Illinois, County of McLean, hereby transfers, conveys, and delivers to the Trustees and their successors the property listed in Schedule "A" or supplemental schedules annexed hereto and incorporated herein by reference, to have and to hold the same, and any cash, securities, or other property which the Trustees may, pursuant to any of the provisions hereof, at any time hereafter hold or acquire, all of such property being hereinafter referred to collectively as the "Trust Estate" for the uses and purposes and upon the terms and conditions herein set forth.

ARTICLE II
Disposition During the Life of the Trustor

During the life of the Trustor, the Trustees shall hold, manage, invest, and re-invest the Trust Estate, and shall collect the income thereof and shall dispose of the net income and Principal as follows:

A.   The Trustees shall pay to the Trustor all of the net income of this Trust, in monthly or other convenient installments, but at least annually. The Trustees may, in their discretion, pay or apply for the benefit of the Trustor, in addition to the income payments herein provided for, such amounts of the Principal of the Trust Estate, up to the whole thereof, as the Trustees may from time to time deem necessary or advisable for the use and benefit of the Trustor.

ARTICLE III
Disposition on Death of the Trustor

A.   Upon the death of the Trustor, the property of the trust, and including also any other portions added thereto from the estate of the Trustor or other sources, along with the undistributed income shall be held in trust and shall be administered and disposed of as follows:

B.   The Trustee shall divide the trust estate into one hundred (100) equal shares and shall distribute such shares as follows:

Ralph Hall, son, and Bryce Hall, son, a total of	90 shares
Dori Jones, granddaughter,	2 shares
Jonathan Hall, grandson,	2 shares
Matthew Hall, grandson,	2 shares
Jessica Lewis, niece,	2 shares
Presbyterian Church of Fair Oaks	2 shares
TOTAL	100 shares

The total of 90 shares appointed to sons Ralph Hall and Bryce Hall shall be divided between them in an equitable and fair manner using the following concept and formula (actual amounts, of course, will differ):

(1)   Trust Estate Assets Equal to 90 Shares:

Real Property	$200,000
Stocks and Bonds	$100,000
Life Insurance	$ 50,000
Personal Property	$ 50,000
TOTAL	$400,000

(2)   Total Amount for Adjustment and Distribution Purposes:

Trust Estate Assets (90 shares)	$400,000
Gifts and Unpaid Balances of Loans Made to Grantor's Sons and Their Families (Schedule "D")	$200,000
TOTAL DISTRIBUTION AMOUNT	$600,000

Gifts and unpaid balances of loans made to Grantor's sons and their families are included in Schedule "D" which is hereby made a part of the Trust. This Schedule "D" is a permanent record of the value of gifts – excluding holiday, birthday, and low-value gifts – and unpaid and forgiven balances of loans made to Grantor's sons and their families. This record shall be maintained on a current basis and shall include the date, amount, and purpose of each gift, unpaid loan balances and loan forgiven amounts. The total amount for each son for each year shall be calculated. Schedule "D" records shall be filed with a copy of the Trust in the asset file. An acceptable format is shown in Example 6-5.

(3)   Adjusted Share of Trust Estate Assets:

Average amount for each son ($600,000 ÷ 2), $300,000
Adjustment for each son:
Ralph Hall, $300,000 less $120,000 from Schedule "D", $180,000.
Bryce Hall, $300,000 less $80,000 from Schedule "D", $220,000.

(4)   Adjusted Distribution of 90 Shares of Trust Estate Assets:

Ralph Hall,	$180,000
Bryce Hall,	$220,000
TOTAL	$400,000

Individual beneficiaries will receive their portion of the trust estate as follows: at the age of Twenty-one (21).

C.   If any of the beneficiaries in Article III, paragraph B, who are individuals, shall be deceased, then the Trustees shall divide the shares or part for the deceased beneficiary into as many equal shares as may be necessary to provide one part or share for the then living descendants of the deceased beneficiary, they taking *per stirpes*; and as thusly divided, each said share or part shall be held as a separate trust for the benefit of the person or persons for whom it was set aside and shall be held, administered, and distributed as follows:

1. The Trustees may use and expend or apply so much or all of, first, the income, and second, the principal of the trusts hereby created for the benefit of a beneficiary hereof, and said amounts shall be used as the Trustees determine necessary or advisable and in such reasonable manner as the Trustees see fit, to provide for the health, reasonable comfort, education, support, and maintenance of the beneficiary for whom such trust shall have been created. Provided, however, that in determining said amounts the Trustees shall first take into account the needs, assets, and other available sources of income and support of a beneficiary thereof. Provided, further, however, the said powers of encroachments upon the beneficiary's share shall be limited to the respective shares held for the respective beneficiary.

2. As and when a beneficiary shall meet the requirements designated in paragraph B, above, the Trustees shall distribute to said respective beneficiary the share of the Trust estate for him or her, free and clear of trust.

3. In the event a beneficiary is for any reason unable or unwilling to take any portion of his share of the Trust Estate pursuant to the above *paragraphs of this Article III*, then such portion shall be distributed to his or her living descendants equally, they taking *per stirpes*, and if there be no such descendants, then such funds shall be equally divided between such beneficiary's then-living brothers and sisters, and if there be no brother or sister then living, then such funds shall be divided equally between the descendants of such beneficiary's brothers and sisters, they taking *per stripes*, and if there be no descendants of such beneficiary's brothers or sisters then living, then the Trustees shall add that portion of the property of that beneficiary to the other portions of the other living beneficiaries, and if there are no other living beneficiaries then: distribution shall be made according to the Illinois law of intestate succession, as in force on the date of the signing of this Trust Agreement. Notwithstanding anything contained to the contrary in this paragraph, if, under the provisions of this *subparagraph 3., of paragraph C., Article III*, any person who does not yet meet the requirements designated in paragraph B, above, shall become entitled to a share of the Trust Estate, such share shall not be distributed to such beneficiary, but shall be retained in trust for said beneficiary's benefit, and shall be held, administered, and disposed of according to *subparagraphs 1., 2., and 3., of paragraph C., Article III*.

4. If under the terms of this Article III, upon the death of any beneficiary, any other person for whom a share or portion is being held in trust shall become entitled to an additional share or portion, such additional share or portion shall not be delivered free of trust, but shall be added to the principal of the share or portion held in trust for such person and shall go as and with the same.

5. At the death of the Trustor, the Trustees shall distribute all of the Trustor's personal effects or other assets, including any contents of the Trustor's residence, to the persons named in one

or more letters of instructions, entitled "Disposition of Personal Effects" referring to *Article III., Subparagraph C.,* of this Trust Agreement, dated and signed by the Trustor and located among the Trustor's important papers at the time of his or her death. In the event that the Trustor has inadvertently named two or more persons to take a particular item, then the most recently dated letter of instruction shall control.

6. If any beneficiary named in paragraph B, above, is an organization, and such organization does not exist at the time of the death of the Trustor, then, if the organization was a charitable institution, the share designated for that charitable organization shall be distributed to another organization, chosen by the trustees, who has similar purposes and functions as the charitable organization that no longer exists. If the organization was not a charitable institution then the share designated for such organization shall be added back to the balance of the trust estate and divided to the other beneficiaries named in paragraph B, above.

7. A trustee in his discretion may terminate and distribute any trust hereunder if the trustee determines that the costs of continuance thereof will substantially impair accomplishment of the purposes of the trust. The trustee shall terminate and forthwith distribute any trust created hereby, or by exercise of a power of appointment hereunder. Distribution under this section shall be made to the persons then entitled to receive or have the benefit of the income from the trust in the proportions in which they are entitled thereto, or if their interests are indefinite, then in equal shares.

D.   Whenever used herein, the term "issue", "child", "children", and "descendants" include adopted issue, adopted child, adopted children, and adopted descendants, as well as natural issue, natural child, natural children, and natural descendants, and include descendants of adopted issue, adopted child, adopted children, and adopted descendants. Provided, however, adopted issue who are also natural issue shall take their share of the Trust Estate only in one capacity, such capacity being the one which grants to such issue the larger share. Where applicable, the masculine includes the feminine, and vice versa, and the neuter includes the masculine or feminine, and vice versa. Where applicable, the singular includes the plural and vice versa.

ARTICLE IV
Spendthrift Provision

No beneficiary of this trust, other than a Trustor, shall have any right to alienate, encumber of hypothecate his/her interest in the trust to claims of his/her creditors, or to render such interest liable to attachment, execution, or other process of law. The income of this trust shall not be pledged, assigned, transferred, sold or accelerated, anticipated or encumbered in any manner whatsoever by any beneficiary, nor shall any income of the trust be in any manner subject or liable in the hands of the Trustees for the debts, contractors or encroachments of any beneficiary or be subject to any assignments or any other voluntary or involuntary alienation or disposition whatsoever. If the creditor of any beneficiary, other than a Trustor, who is entitled to any distributions from a trust established under this instrument shall attempt by any means to subject to the satisfaction of his claim such beneficiary's interest in distribution, then, notwithstanding any other provision herein, until the release of the writ of attachment or garnishment or other process, the distribution set aside for such beneficiary shall be disposed of as follows:

1. Distribution to Beneficiary. The Trustees shall pay to or apply for the benefit of such beneficiary such sums as the Trustees shall determine to be necessary for the reasonable health, education (including study at institutions of higher learning) and support of the beneficiary according to his or her accustomed mode of life.

2. Disposition of Excess. The portion of the distribution that the Trustees shall determine to be in excess of the amount necessary for such health, education (including study at institutions of higher learning) and support shall be added to and become principal of the trust share of such beneficiary and will be paid to said beneficiary or subsequent heirs in a manner to maximize the benefit to the beneficiary without compromise of the intent of this trust to provide an inheritance to the heirs.

ARTICLE V
Invalid Provisions

If any provisions of this trust are held to be invalid, none of the other provisions shall be thereby rendered invalid or inoperative as long as the remaining Trust Agreement does not frustrate the intents of the Trustor, but tends to accomplish his or her overall objectives.

ARTICLE VI
Perpetuities Savings Clause

In any event, and anything to the contrary herein contained notwithstanding, the trusts created in this agreement shall terminate upon the day next preceding the expiration of twenty-one (21) years after the death of the Trustor and their issue now living, in the event these trusts shall not have previously terminated in accordance with the terms hereof. In the event of termination of these trusts as provided for in this paragraph, the Trustees shall distribute the Trust Estate as it shall then be constituted, together with any new income, to the beneficiaries then entitled to the income from the Trust Estate in the same proportions in which they are entitled to such income.

ARTICLE VII
Trustees

A.   The following people will act as Trustees in the following order of succession:

First. Edna Mae Hall

Second. At the death of the Trustor, the following, shall serve as successor Trustees, in the order listed: **Richard A. Smith, and then Karen Jones**. The executor for the heirs is **Richard A. Smith,** who may speak on behalf of any minor beneficiaries.

Third. Trustee(s) chosen by a majority of the beneficiaries, with a parent or legal guardian voting for minor beneficiaries; provided, however, that the issue of any deceased child shall have collectively only one vote.

B.   A majority of the trustees, whether individual or corporate, shall have the power to make any decision, undertake any action, or execute any documents affecting the Trusts created herein. In the event of a difference of opinion among the Trustees, the decision of a majority of them shall prevail, but the dissenting or nonassenting trustees shall not be responsible for any action taken by the majority pursuant to such decisions. If only two individual Trustees are in office, they must act unanimously. If an individual and a corporate Trustee are in office, the determination of the Individual Trustees shall be binding.

C. Any Trustees may from time to time delegate to one or more of the remaining Trustees any powers, duties, or discretions. Every such delegation shall be made by a writing delivered to the delegate or delegates, and shall remain effective for the time therein specified or until earlier revocation by a writing similarly delivered. Every one dealing with the Trustees shall be absolutely protected in relying upon the certificate of any Trustees as to who are the Trustee(s) for the time being acting, and as to the extent of their authority by reason of any delegation or otherwise.

D. No Trustees named above need give bond in any jurisdiction. If a fiduciary's bond may not be dispensed with, the Trustor requests that the bond be accepted without surety and in the lowest possible amount. In the absence of breach of trust, no Trustees shall ever be required to qualify before, be appointed by, or account to any court, or obtain the order or approval of any court in the exercise of any power or discretion herein given. The Trustees are entitled to ordinary and reasonable compensation for services rendered in the administration and distribution of the estate.

ARTICLE VIII
Powers of the Trustees

A. The Trustees shall have full power to do everything in administering these trusts that they deem for the best interests of the beneficiaries (whether or not it be authorized or appropriate for fiduciaries but for this broad grant of authority), including power:

1. To acquire by purchase or otherwise, and to retain so long as they deem advisable, any kind of realty or personal property, or undivided interests therein, including common and preferred stocks, bonds, or other unsecured obligations, options, warrants interests in investment trusts and discretionary common trust funds, all without diversification as to kind or amount, without being limited to investments authorized by law for the investment of trust funds, and power to hold or take title to property in the name of a nominee.

2. To sell for cash or on credit, at private or public sale, exchange, hypothecate, sell short, or otherwise dispose of any real or personal property.

3. To make distributions, including distributions to themselves as Trustees, in kind or in money or partly in each, even if shares be composed differently; for such purposes, the valuation of the Trustees shall be given effect if reasonably made.

4. If, in the Trustees' discretion, any beneficiary (whether a minor or of legal age) in incapable of making proper disposition of any sum of income or principal that is payable or appointed to said beneficiary under the terms of this Trust Agreement, the Trustees may apply said sum to or on behalf of the beneficiary by any one with whom the beneficiary resides, or by payments in discharge of the beneficiary's bills or debts, including bills for premiums on any insurance policies, or by paying an allowance to a beneficiary directly. The foregoing payments shall be made without regard to other resources of the beneficiary, or the duty of any person to support the beneficiary and without the intervention of any guardian or like fiduciary; provided, however, that the Trustees shall ensure and see to the application of the funds for the benefit of the beneficiary, so that the funds will not be used by any adult

person, or any other person for a purpose other than the direct benefit of the beneficiary, and particularly so that said funds will not be diverted for the purpose of support and education of said beneficiary.

5. To determine whether and to what extent receipts should be deemed income or principal, whether or to what extent expenditures should be charged against principal or income, and what other adjustments should be made between principal and income, provided such adjustments do not conflict with well-settled rules for the determination of principal and income questions.

6. To delegate powers to agents including accountants, investment counsel, appraisers, legal counsel, and other experts, remunerate them and pay their expenses; to employ custodians of the Trust assets, bookkeepers, clerks, and other assistants and pay them out of income or principal.

7. To renew, assign, alter, extend, compromise, release, with or without consideration, or submit to arbitration or litigation, obligations or claims held by or asserted against the Trustor, the Trustees, or the Trust Assets.

8. To borrow money from others for the payment of taxes, debts, or expenses, or for any other purpose which, in the opinion of the Trustees, will facilitate the administration of these trusts, and pledge or mortgage property as security for such loans; and, if money is borrowed from any Trustees, individually, to pay interest thereon at the then-prevailing rate of interest.

9. To lease, or grant options to lease, for periods to begin presently or in the future, without regard to statutory restrictions or the probable duration of any trust; to erect or alter buildings or otherwise improve and manage property; demolish buildings; make ordinary and extraordinary repairs; grant easements and charges; make partywall contracts; dedicate roads, subdivide; adjust boundary lines; partition and convey property or give money for equity of partition; to be either a general or limited partner.

10. To enter into transactions with any other trust in which the Trustor or the beneficiaries of the Trust Agreement, or any of them, have beneficial interests, even though any Trustee of such other trust is also a Trustee under this Trust Agreement.

11. To exercise all the foregoing powers alone or in conjunction with others, even though any of the Trustees are personally interested in the property that is involved, notwithstanding any rules of law relating to divided loyalty or self-dealing.

12. The Trustees may engage in the practice of writing options on all recognized exchanges and buy and sell, on margin or otherwise (including "short" sales), securities of every nature, limited partnerships, and commodities.

13. The Trustees may make gift transactions. However, no Trustee, other than the Trustor acting as Trustee, shall have the power to make gifts, other than to the spouse of the Trustor, if any, in excess of the amount excluded from gift tax under section 2503(b) of the Internal Revenue Code of 1986, as amended, or any successor thereto. No Trustees, other than the Trustor acting as Trustee, shall be authorized to make gifts to charities except in satisfaction of a written pledge of the Trustor. No Trustee, other than the Trustor acting as Trustee, shall be authorized to make gifts to any person who is not a descendant of the Trustor or a beneficiary under this Trust or of the Last Will and Testament of the Trustor, or the spouse of such descendant or beneficiary.

B.   Any Trustee may decline to act or may resign as Trustee at any time by delivering a written resignation to the beneficiaries of a trust then subsisting.

C.   From the income of the trusts hereby created, or, if that be insufficient, from the principal thereof, the Trustees shall pay and discharge all expenses incurred in the administration of the Trusts.

D.   No successor Trustees shall be liable for any misfeasance of any prior Trustees.

ARTICLE IX
Delegation of Authority

During physical or mental incapacitation, the Trustor herein appoints the successor trustees, during said period of incapacitation. The successor trustees will act as Trustee, Guardian, Executor, or in any other legal capacity, whether appointed orally or in writing, and supervise all matters in which the Trustor had the right to act if he or she had not become incapacitated. Incapacitation shall be established either by a court of competent jurisdiction or by a written statement filed with the Trustees and signed in good faith by two (2) physicians unrelated to the Trustor or the beneficiaries. During any period of incapacity or incompetency of the Trustor the Trust is irrevocable and unamendable in regard to its operation or disposition for the affected Trustor. If the Trustor regains competency, the trust will again become amendable and revocable.

ARTICLE X
Additions to Trust

A.   It is understood that the Trustor or any other person may grant, and the Trustees may receive, as part of this Trust, additional real and personal property, by assignment, transfer, deed, or other conveyance, or by any other means, testamentary or inter vivos, for inclusion in the Trust herein created. Any such property so received by the Trustees shall become a part of the Trust and shall become subject to the terms of this Agreement.

B.   It is specifically the intention of the Trustor that all real and personal properties now owned by the Trustor are to be a part of this Trust; provided further, that all future real and personal properties acquired by the Trustor are to be a part of or to automatically become a part of this Trust at the time acquired by the Trustor.

ARTICLE XI
Parties Dealing With Trustees

No purchaser, and no issuer of any stock, bond or other instrument evidencing a deposit of money or property, or other person dealing with the Trustees hereunder with respect to any property hereunder as purchaser, lessee, party to a contract or lease, or in any capacity whatsoever, shall be under any obligation whatsoever to see to the disbursing of money paid to the Trustees or to the due execution of this Trust, in any particular, but such persons shall be absolutely free in dealing with the Trustees on the same basis as though the Trustee(s) were the absolute owner of the said property, without any conditions, restrictions, or qualifications whatsoever.

ARTICLE XII
Revocation and Amendment

A.   As long as the Trustor is alive, the right is reserved to amend, modify, revoke, or remove from this Trust any and all property, in whole or in part, including the principal, and the present or past undisbursed income from such principal. On the death of the Trustor, the remainder of the Trust Estate, and the trusts created hereinafter, may not be amended, revoked, or terminated, other than by disposition of the trust property to the beneficiaries according to the terms stated herein.

B.   While the Trustor is alive, full authority is retained, in his/her discretion, to sell, convey, or mortgage property, without disclosing their capacity as Trustees of this Trust Agreement; any such sale or conveyance of property in accordance with this provision, shall be considered as, and shall cause, a partial, revocation of the Trust with respect to the property so conveyed or sold, and shall be sufficient to remove said property from the Trust.

ARTICLE XIII
Vested Interest of Beneficiaries

The interest of the beneficiaries is a present vested interest which shall continue until this Trust is revoked or terminated other than by death.

ARTICLE XIV
Governing Law

This Agreement shall be construed and regulated by laws of the State of Illinois.

ARTICLE XV
Catastrophic Illness

Should a catastrophic illness occur to the Trustor while living, the successor trustees shall manage the Trust Estate to the greatest advantage to the beneficiaries.

Catastrophic illness shall be defined as an illness that renders the Trustor incompetent or not capable of caring for himself or herself such that full-time care is required, and it is reasonably anticipated that such care shall be needed for a period of six months or longer.

Upon the implementation of the provisions of this article, other provisions not withstanding, the Trust shall become an "income only" Trust, in which none of the corpus of the Trust shall be distributed to the Trustor during the time of the catastrophic illness, but will be held for the benefit of the Trustor, in anticipation of his recovery from the catastrophic illness.

ARTICLE XVI
In Terrorem

In the event that any beneficiary under this trust shall, singly or in conjunction with any other person or persons, contest in any court the validity of this trust or of a deceased Co-Trustor's Last Will or shall seek to obtain an adjudication in any proceeding in any court that this trust or any of its provisions, or that such Will or any of its provisions, is void, or seek otherwise to void, nullify, or set aside this trust or any of its provisions, then the right of that person to take any interest given to him by this trust shall be determined as it would have been determined had the person predeceased the execution of this Trust Agreement. The Trustees are authorized to defend, at the expense of the trust estate, any contest or other attack of any nature on this trust or any of its provisions.

ARTICLE XVII
Attorney Representation

The attorney of record for the preparation of this trust is **John C. Roberts,** of Roberts Assurance Group. If assistance or instruction concerning this trust is required, the Trustor requests that the Trustee(s) call **John C. Roberts,** or another attorney knowledgeable in Estate Planning.

ARTICLE XVIII
Prepared In Duplicate

This Trust Agreement has been prepared in duplicate, each copy of which has been executed as an original. One of these executed copies is in the possession of the Trustor, and the other is deposited for safekeeping with the Trustor's Attorney, **John C. Roberts**. Either copy may be used as the original without the other; if only one copy of this Trust Agreement can be found, then it shall be considered as the original, and the missing copy will be presumed inadvertently lost. Any clarifications or instructions concerning this Trust Agreement may be obtained by calling the above-mentioned attorney, who is requested to do everything necessary to implement the provisions of this Trust.

Example 6-2²*

"Pour Over" LAST WILL AND TESTAMENT
of
Edna Mae Hall

I, Edna Mae Hall, a resident of Normal, Illinois, being of sound and disposing mind and memory and over the age of eighteen years, do hereby declare this to be my Last Will and Testament, and I expressly revoke all Wills, including codicils, heretofore made by me.

ARTICLE I

1.1   I hereby declare that at the time of making this Last Will and Testament that I am widow.

1.2   I declare that I have two children at this time: Ralph and Bryce

ARTICLE II

2.1   I declare the entire residue of my estate to the Trustee(s) then in office under that trust designated as "The Edna Mae Hall Trust" established March 12, 1996 of which I am the grantor. I direct that the residue of my estate shall be added to, administered, and distributed as part of that trust, according to the terms of the trust and any amendment made to it before my death. To the extent permitted by law, it is not my intent to create a separate trust by this will or to subject the trust or the property added to it by this will to the jurisdiction of the probate court.

2.2   I hereby direct that my Executor or my Trustee(s) may elect to: (1) use administrative expenses as deduction either for estate tax purposes or income tax purposes; and (2) to use either date of death values or optional values for estate tax purposes, regardless of the effect thereof on any of the interests under this Will.

2.3   I further direct that my Executor or Trustee(s) shall not be required to pay any debt in advance of the due date thereof, including installment obligations, but instead may pay the same in installments as each installment comes due. However if the Trustee(s) deem it to the advantage of the estate any or all debts may be paid in advance of their required installments.

2.4   I stipulate that any asset under litigation, lien, or claim that might cause the assets of the aforementioned Trust to be compromised in any fashion, be held separate from the said Trust until it is free of any claim or threat to the integrity of the Trust.

ARTICLE III

3.1   If the disposition in Article II, above, is inoperative or is invalid for any reason, or if the trust referred to in Article II above, fails or is revoked, I incorporate the terms of that trust herein by reference, as if executed on this date, without giving effect to any amendments made subsequently, and I bequeath and devise the residue of my estate to the Trustee(s) named in the trust as Trustee(s), to be held, administered, and distributed as provided in that instrument.

Signed _____

---

² * Pages 6-46 through 6-53

ARTICLE IV

4.1   I do hereby nominate the following individual(s) as the Executor(s) of this Will, to serve in the order listed: Richard A. Smith, Karen Jones.

4.2   The Executor shall have full power and authority to carry out the provisions of the Will, including the power to manage and operate during the probate of my estate any property and any business belonging to my estate. However, the Executor should not compromise the referenced trust in any fashion by premature transfer of assets that may carry any claim or litigation into the Trust.

4.3   The Executor or Trustee(s) shall serve without bond. However, in the event that one (1) or more bonds are required for one (1) or more such individuals, in their capacities as Executors hereunder, then I request that such bonds be nominal bonds, and, my Executor shall pay any such bond premiums, as bonds premiums are due, as administration expenses of my estate, until the administration of my estate is completed.

IN WITNESS WHEREOF, I have hereunto subscribed my name to this document, my last Will and Testament, which consists of four (4) typewritten pages, and for the purpose of identification, I have initialed or signed each page, all in the presence of the persons who are witnessing, at my request, the execution of this, my last Will and Testament on this _____ day of _____ , _____ , at _____ , _____ .

_____

Edna Mae Hall

Signed _____

Example 6-3[3*]

Certificate of Acknowledgement of Notary Public

State of Illinois)

   :ss.

County of McLean)

   On this _____ day of _____, A.D. 19 _____, appeared before me Edna Mae Hall personally known to me (or proved to me on the basis of satisfactory evidence) to be the person whose name is subscribed in this instrument, and acknowledged that he/she executed it.

_____   Residing in _____

Notary Public

My Commission Expires _____

NOTARY SEAL:

Signed _____

---

[3] * Pages 6-53 through 6-67

LAST WILL AND TESTAMENT
WITNESS PAGE:

We, the undersigned, do hereby certify that Edna Mae Hall on this _____ day of _____, 20_____, declared the above and foregoing instrument, consisting of four (4) pages, each of which is signed by Edna Mae Hall, to be his/her Last Will and Testament, and that thereupon he/she asked us to act as witnesses to such Will, and did in the presence of each of us sign his/her name to such Will; that, thereupon, we and each of us, in the presence of Edna Mae Hall and in the presence of each other, do sign our names as witnesses to such Will.

_____ (Witness Signature) _____ Date
_____ (Print Name)
_____ (Address)
_____ (City, State, Zip Code)

_____ (Witness Signature) _____ Date
_____ (Print Name)
_____ (Address)
_____ (City, State, Zip Code)

Signed _____

ACKNOWLEDGEMENT OF THE EXECUTION OF
THE LAST WILL AND TESTAMENT OF Edna Mae Hall

We, whose names are signed below, each declare under penalties of perjury: that Edna Mae Hall, the testator, executed the foregoing instrument as the testator's last will and testament; that in our presence, the testator signed the testator's signature and declared that such signing was the testator's free and voluntary act for the purpose of executing the testator's last will and testament; that each of the Witnesses thereto, in the presence of the testator (and at the testator's request) and in the presence of each other, signed such instrument which the testator stated to be the testator's last will and testament; and, to the best of our knowledge, the testator was, at the time of the testator's signing and at the time of the signing of the witnesses, eighteen (18) or more years of age and sound of mind.

_____

Edna Mae Hall

_____ (Witness Signature) _____ Date
_____ (Print Name)
_____ (Address)
_____ (City, State, Zip Code)

_____ (Witness Signature) _____ Date
_____ (Print Name)
_____ (Address)
_____ (City, State, Zip Code)

Certificate of Copy of Will

IN THE CIRCUIT COURT 11ᵀᴴ JUDICIAL CIRCUIT, McLEAN COUNTY, ILLINOIS

STATE OF ILLINOIS,

    }   ss.

McLean County,   I, the undersigned Circuit Clerk, in and for the said County, in the State aforesaid (the said Court being a Court of Record and having a seal), do hereby certify that the annexed instrument in writing is a true Copy of the last Will and Testament of <u>Edna Mae Hall</u> deceased, as proven and admitted to record in the said Court, on the _____ day of _____, AD. 20_____ as appears from the Records of said Court in my Office, Probate Division.

Given under my hand and the seal of said Court, at Bloomington, said County, this _____ day of _____, A.D. 20_____

_____ Clerk.

By _____Deputy.

Example 6-3[4]*

RECORDING REQUESTED BY
EDWIN BOLTON JONES, JR.
7605 Palisade Way
Fair Oaks, CA 95628
WHEN RECORDED, MAIL TO:
SAME AS ABOVE   SPACE ABOVE FOR RECORDER'S USE

SPRINGING DURABLE POWER OF ATTORNEY

A.   PRINCIPAL: **EDWIN BOLTON JONES, JR.**
B.   ATTORNEY-IN-FACT APPOINTED: **PATRICIA YVONNE JONES**

WARNING TO PERSON EXECUTING THIS DOCUMENT:

This is an important legal document. It creates a durable power of attorney that becomes effective on your incapacity as hereafter set forth. Before executing this document, you should know these important facts.

1.   This document may provide the person you designate as your Attorney-In-Fact with broad powers to dispose, sell convey and encumber your real and personal property.
2.   These powers will exist for an indefinite period of time unless you limit their duration in this document. These powers will continue to exist notwithstanding your subsequent disability or incapacity.
3.   You have the right to revoke or terminate this Durable Power of Attorney at any time.

---

[4] * Pages 6-54 through 6-68

POWER OF ATTORNEY TO BECOME EFFECTIVE
ONLY ON INCAPACITY OF PRINCIPAL

This Durable Power of Attorney shall become effective only on the incapacity of the undersigned principal. The undersigned shall conclusively be deemed incapacitated for purposes of this instrument when the Attorney-In-Fact receives a written and signed opinion from two (2) licensed physicians that the principal is physically or mentally incapable of managing his/her finances. Such written opinion when received shall be attached to this instrument. Third parties may rely on the Attorney-In-Fact's authority without further evidence of incapacity when this instrument is presented with such physicians' statement attached. The principal hereby waives any privilege that may apply to the release of information included in such medical opinion.

While the principal is not incapacitated, this Durable Power of Attorney may be modified by the principal at any time by written notice given by the principal to the Attorney-In-Fact and may be terminated at any time by either the principal or the Attorney-In-Fact by written notice given by the terminating party to the other party.

This Durable Power of Attorney shall continue after the principal's incapacity in accordance with its terms.

On the death of the principal, this Durable Power of Attorney shall terminate and the assets of the principal shall be distributed to the duly appointed personal representative of the principal's estate; or, if no estate is being administered, to the persons who lawfully take the assets without the necessity of administration when they have supplied the Attorney-In-Fact with satisfactory documents as provided by law.

HOME SWEET WELL MANAGED HOME

TO WHOM IT MAY CONCERN:

I, **EDWIN BOLTON JONES, JR.,** the principal, presently a resident of Fair Oaks, California, hereby appoint **PATRICIA YVONNE JONES**, presently a resident of Fair Oaks, California, as my true and lawful Attorney-In-Fact for me and in my name, place and stead on my incapacity:

1. REAL PROPERTY: To manage, control, lease, sublease and otherwise act concerning any real property that I may own, collect and receive rents or income therefrom, pay taxes, charges and assessments on the same, repair, maintain, protect, preserve, alter, and improve the same and do all things necessary or expedient to be done in the Attorney-In-Fact's judgment in connection with the property.

2. PARTNERSHIPS: To manage and control all partnerships interests owned by me and to make all decisions I could make as a general partner, limited partner, or both, and to execute all documents required of me as such partner, all to the extent that the Attorney-In-Fact's designation for such purposes is allowed by law and is not in contravention of any partnership or other agreement.

3. BUSINESS INTERESTS: To conduct or participate in any lawful business of whatever nature for me and in my name; incorporate, reorganize, merge, consolidate, recapitalize, sell, liquidate or dissolve any business; elect or employ officers, directors and agents; carry out the provisions of any agreement for the sale of any business interest or the stock therein; and exercise voting rights with respect to stock, either in person or by proxy, and exercise stock options.

4. SECURITIES: To purchase, sell, invest, reinvest and generally deal with all my funds in every kind of property, real, personal, or mixed, and every kind of investment, specifically including but not limited to, corporate obligations of every kind, preferred or common stocks, bonds, debentures, warrants, partnership interests and rights, shares of investment trusts, investment companies, and mutual funds, and mortgage participations that, under the circumstances then prevailing (specifically including but not limited to the general economic conditions and my anticipated needs) that persons of skill, prudence and diligence acting in a similar capacity and familiar with those matters would use in the conduct of an enterprise of a similar character and with similar aims, to attain my goals; and to consider individual investments as part of an overall plan.

5. MOTOR VEHICLES: To apply for a Certificate of Title upon, and endorse or transfer title thereof, for any automobile, truck, pickup, van, motorcycle or other motor vehicle, and to represent in such transfer assignment that the title to said motor vehicle is free and clear of all liens and encumbrances except those specifically set forth in such transfer assignment.

6. ACCOUNTS RECEIVABLE: To collect and deposit for my benefit all debts, interest, dividends, or other assets that may be due or belong to me and to execute and deliver receipts and other discharges therefor; to demand, arbitrate and pursue litigation in my behalf concerning all rights and benefits to which I may be entitled; and to compromise, settle and discharge all such matters as the Attorney-In-Fact considers appropriate under the circumstances.

7. <u>ACCOUNTS PAYABLE:</u> To pay any sums of money that may at any time be or become owing from me, to sell and to adjust and compromise any claims which may be against me as the Attorney-In-Fact considers appropriate under the circumstances.

8. <u>CONVEYANCES:</u> To grant, sell, transfer, mortgage, deed in trust, pledge and otherwise deal in all property, real and personal, that I may own, including but not limited to any real property described on any exhibit attached to this instrument including property acquired after execution of this instrument; to attach exhibits to this instrument that provide legal descriptions of all such property; and to execute such instruments as the Attorney-In-Fact deems proper in conjunction with all matters covered in this paragraph.

9. <u>TAXES:</u> To prepare and file all income and other federal and state tax returns which I am required to file, to sign my name, hire preparers and advisors and pay for their services, and to do whatever is necessary to protect my assets from assessments for income taxes and other taxes. The Attorney-In-Fact is specifically authorized to receive confidential information; to receive checks in payment of any refund of taxes, penalties, or interest; to execute waivers (including offers of waivers) of restrictions on assessment or collection of tax deficiencies and waivers of notice of disallowance of claims for credit or refund; to execute consents extending the statutory period for assessment or collection of taxes; to execute closing agreements under Internal Revenue Code Section 7121 or any successor statute; and to delegate authority or substitute another representative with respect to all of the above matters.

10. <u>DEPOSITORY ACCOUNTS:</u> To deposit in and draw on any checking, savings, agency, or other accounts that I may have in any banks, savings and loan associates, and any accounts with securities brokers or other commercial institutions, and to establish and terminate all such accounts.

11. <u>SAFE DEPOSIT BOXES:</u> To have access to all safe deposit boxes in my name or to which I am an authorized signatory, wheresoever located; to contract with financial institutions for the maintenance and continuation of safe deposit boxes in my name; to add to and remove the contents of all such safety deposit boxes; and to terminate contracts for all such safety deposit boxes.

12. <u>PURCHASE OF BONDS:</u> To purchase for my sole account United States of America Treasury Bonds of any kind which are redeemable at par in payment of federal estate taxes, and to borrow money and obtain credit in my name from any source for such purpose; in connection therewith, to make, execute, endorse and deliver any and all necessary or desirable promissory notes, bills of exchange, drafts, agreements, or other obligations; as security therefore to pledge, mortgage and assign any stock, bonds, securities, insurance values and other properties, real and personal, which I may own or in which I may have an interest; and to arrange for the safekeeping and custody of any such Treasury Bonds.

13. <u>REVOCABLE TRUSTS:</u> To make additions and transfer assets to any and all living revocable trusts created by me, any or all assets not or at any time or times hereafter standing in my name or representing my interest in assets owned jointly, commonly or otherwise with ownership rights in insurance policies of all kinds, cash checks (particularly government and insurance checks), stocks, bonds (including any purchases under paragraph 12 above), securities and properties of all kinds; and pursuant to such purpose to terminate savings, checking safekeeping, agency, investment advisory and custody accounts in my name alone

or with others, at any bank or broker, by directing that all or any part of the balance therein, including all cash, stocks, bonds and other securities and property, subject to any indebtedness secured thereby, be transferred and delivered to said Trustee or Trustees.

14. <u>CHILDREN:</u> To make direct payments to the provider for tuition and medical care for my issue under Internal Revenue Code Section 2503(e) or any successor statute, which excludes such payments from gift tax liability.

15. <u>CREDIT CARDS:</u> To use any credit cards in my name to make necessary purchases for my benefit and to sign charge slips on behalf of me as may be required to use such credit cards; and to close my charge accounts and terminate my credit cards under circumstances where the Attorney-In-Fact considers such acts to be in my best interest.

16. <u>GENERAL POWERS:</u> Generally to do, execute and perform any other act, deed, matter, or thing, that in the opinion of the Attorney-In-Fact ought to be done, executed, or performed in conjunction with this Durable Power of Attorney, of every kind and nature, as fully and effectively as I could do if personally present. The enumeration of specific items, acts, rights, or powers does not limit or restrict, and is not be construed or interpreted as limiting or restricting, the general powers granted to the Attorney-In-Fact except where powers are expressly restricted.

17. <u>ENFORCEMENT:</u> The Attorney-In-Fact is authorized and directed to commence enforcement proceedings, at my expense, against any third party who fails to honor this Durable Power of Attorney.

18. <u>RESTRICTIONS:</u> Notwithstanding any other possible language to the contrary in this document, the Attorney-In-Fact is specifically <u>NOT</u> granted the following powers:

A. To use my assets for the Attorney-In-Fact's own legal obligations, including but not limited to support of the Attorney-In-Fact's dependents; and

B. To exercise any trustee powers under an irrevocable trust of which the Attorney-In-Fact is a trustor and the principal is a trustee; and

C. To exercise incidents of ownership over any life insurance policies that I own on the Attorney-In-Fact's life.

1. <u>INFORMATION FROM THIRD PARTIES:</u> Any third party from whom the Attorney-In-Fact may request information, records, or other documents regarding my personal affairs may release and deliver all such information, records, or documents to the Attorney-In-Fact. I hereby waive any privilege that may apply to the release of such information, record, or other documents.

2. <u>THIRD PARTY RELIANCE:</u> The Attorney-In-Fact's signature under the authority granted in this durable Power of Attorney may be accepted by any third party or organization with the same force and effect as if I were personally present and acting in my own behalf. No person or organization who relies on the Attorney-In-Fact's authority under this instrument shall incur any liability to me, my estate, heirs, successors, or assigns, because of reliance on this instrument.

3. <u>HEIRS:</u> My estate, heirs, successors and assigns shall be bound by the Attorney-In-Fact's act under this Durable Power of Attorney.

4. <u>EFFECTIVE DATE:</u> This Durable Power of Attorney shall commence and take effect on my subsequent disability or incapacity as set forth above.

5. <u>CONSERVATORSHIP:</u> If a conservatorship of my person or estate or both is deemed necessary, I hereby nominate **PATRICIA YVONNE JONES** as conservator of my person and estate. I grant to my conservator all the powers specified in the California Probate Code. My conservator shall serve in such capacity without bond, or if a bond is required, I request that such bond be set as low as possible. If **PATRICIA YVONNE JONES** is for any reason unwilling or unable to serve, I hereby nominate the following person to serve as the alternate conservator:

Name: **ANNE LOUISE RILEY**
Address: (Fill-in complete address)
City, State and Zip Code:
Telephone Number:

If the above-named person is for any reason unwilling or unable to so serve as the alternate conservator, then I hereby nominate the following person to serve as the alternate conservator:

Name: **SCOTT ALAN JONES**
Address: (Fill-in complete address)
City, State and Zip Code:
Telephone Number:

On the appointment of a conservator of my estate, this Durable Power of Attorney shall terminate and the Attorney-In-Fact shall deliver my assets under the Attorney-In-Fact's control as directed by the conservator of my estate.

6. <u>SUCCESSOR ATTORNEY-IN-FACT:</u> If **PATRICIA YVONNE JONES** is for any reason unwilling or unable to serve as my Attorney-In-Fact, to make decisions for me as authorized in this document, I hereby nominate the following:

Name: **ANNE LOUISE RILEY**
Address: (Fill-in complete address)
City, State and Zip Code:
Telephone Number:

If the above-named person is for any reason unwilling or unable to so serve as my Attorney-In-Fact, then I hereby appoint the following person to serve as the alternate Attorney-In-Fact, to make decisions for me as authorized in this document:

Name: **SCOTT ALAN JONES**
Address: (Fill-in complete address)
City, State and Zip Code:
Telephone Number:

7. <u>EXCULPATION:</u> No Attorney-In-Fact named herein or substituted herein shall incur any liability to me for acting or refraining from acting hereunder, except for such Attorney-In-Fact's own willful misconduct or gross negligence.

8. <u>SEVERABILITY:</u> If any provision of this Durable Power of Attorney is not enforceable or is not valid, the remaining provisions shall remain effective.

9. <u>GOVERNING LAW:</u> This Durable Power of Attorney shall be governed by the laws of the State of California in all respects, including its validity, construction, interpretation and termination.

10. <u>RATIFICATION:</u> As the principal, I hereby ratify and confirm all that the Attorney-In-Fact shall do or cause to be done by virtue of this Durable Power of Attorney, and all such promissory notes, bills of exchange, drafts, other obligations, agreements, stock powers, instruments and documents, signed, endorsed, drawn, accepted, made, executed, or delivered by the said Attorney-In-Fact, or any substitute or substitutes of said Attorney-In-Fact, which shall hereafter be received, shall bind me and my heirs, distributees, legal representative, successors and assigns.

IN WITNESS WHEREOF, as the principal, I sign this Durable Power of Attorney this _____ day of _____, in the year of 20_____.

_____

EDWIN BOLTON JONES, JR.

CERTIFICATE OF ACKNOWLEDGEMENT OF NOTARY PUBLIC

STATE OF CALIFORNIA
COUNTY OF _____

On this _____ day of _____, in the year 20_____, before me, the undersigned Notary Public, personally appeared **EDWIN BOLTON JONES, JR.,** personally known to me (or proved to me on the basis of satisfactory evidence) to be the person whose name is sworn and subscribed to this instrument, and acknowledged that he/she executed it.

I declare under penalty of perjury that the person whose name is subscribed to the instrument appears to be of sound mind and under no duress, fraud or under influence.

_____

Notary Public, State of California
(Seal)
My Commission Expires: _____

DURABLE POWER OF ATTORNEY FOR HEALTH CARE DECISIONS

Example 6-4

6-69

DURABLE POWER OF ATTORNEY FOR HEALTH CARE DECISIONS
Example 6-4

WARNING TO PERSON EXECUTING THIS DOCUMENT

This is an important legal document. Before executing this document, you should know these important facts:

This document gives the person you designate as your agent (the attorney-in-fact) the power to make health care decisions for you. Your agent must act consistently with your desires as stated in this document or otherwise made known.

Except as you otherwise specify in this document, this document gives your agent power to consent to your doctor not giving treatment or stopping treatment necessary to keep you alive.

Notwithstanding this document, you have the right to make medical and other health care decisions for yourself so long as you can give informed consent with respect to the particular decision. In addition, no treatment may be given to you over your objection, and health care necessary to keep you alive may not be stopped or withheld if you object at the time.

This document gives your agent authority to consent, to refuse to consent, or to withdraw consent to any care, treatment, service, or procedure to maintain, diagnose, or treat a physical or mental condition. This power is subject to any statement of your desires and any limitations that you include in this document. You may state in this document any types of treatment that you do not desire. In addition, a court can take away the power of your agent to make health care decisions for you if your agent (1) authorizes anything that is illegal, (2) acts contrary to your known desires or (3) where your desires are not known, does anything that is clearly contrary to your best interests.

This power will exist for an indefinite period of time unless you limit its duration in this document.

You have the right to revoke the authority of your agent by notifying your agent or your treating doctor, hospital, or other health care provider orally or in writing of the revocation.

Your agent has the right to examine your medical records and to consent to their disclosure unless you limit this right in this document.

Unless you otherwise specify in this document, this document gives your agent the power after you die to (1) authorize an autopsy, (2) donate your body or parts thereof for transplant or therapeutic or educational or scientific purposes, and (3) direct the disposition of your remains.

If there is anything in this document that you do not understand, you should ask a lawyer to explain it to you.

---

1. CREATION OF DURABLE POWER OF ATTORNEY FOR HEALTH CARE

By this document I intend to create a durable power of attorney by appointing the person designated below to make health care decisions for me as allowed by Sections 2410 to 2444, inclusive, of the   (*)   This power of attorney shall not be affected by my subsequent incapacity. I hereby revoke any prior durable power of attorney for health care. I am a who is at least 18 years old, of sound mind, and acting of my own free will.

2. APPOINTMENT OF HEALTH CARE AGENT

(Fill in below the name, address and telephone number of the person you wish to make health care decisions for you if you become incapacitated. You should make sure that this person agrees to accept this responsibility. The following may not serve as your agent: (1) your treating health care provider; (2) an operator of a community care facility or residential care facility for the elderly; or (3) an employee of your treating health care provider, a community care facility, or a residential care facility for the elderly, unless that employee is related to you by blood, marriage or adoption. If you are a conservatee under the Lanterman-Petris-Short Act (the law governing involuntary commitment to a mental health facility) and you wish to appoint your conservator as your agent, you must consult a lawyer, who must sign and attach a special declaration for this document to be valid.)

I, _____ Edwin Bolton Jones, Jr _____, hereby appoint:
(insert your name)

Name _____ Patricia Yvonne Jones _____

Address _____ 1234 Maple Lane, Fair Oaks, Ca 95678 _____

Work Telephone (_____) _____   Home Telephone (__XXX__) X XX-XXXX _____

as my agent (attorney-in-fact) to make health care decisions for me as authorized in this document. I understand that this power of attorney will be effective for an indefinite period of time unless I revoke it or limit its duration below.

(Optional) This power of attorney shall expire on the following date: _December 31, 2020_____.

   * Enter name of State   /

3. AUTHORITY OF AGENT

If I become incapable of giving informed consent to health care decisions, I grant my agent full power and authority to make those decisions for me, subject to any statements of desires or limitations set forth below. Unless I have limited my agent's authority in this document, that authority shall include the right to consent, refuse consent, or withdraw consent to any medical care, treatment, service, or procedure; to receive and to consent to the release of medical information; to authorize an autopsy to determine the cause of my death; to make a gift of all or part of my body; and to direct the disposition of my remains, subject to any instructions I have given in a written contract for funeral services, my will or by some other method. I understand that, by law, my agent may **not** consent to any of the following: commitment to a mental health treatment facility, convulsive treatment, psychosurgery, sterilization or abortion.

4. MEDICAL TREATMENT DESIRES AND LIMITATIONS (OPTIONAL)

(Your agent must make health care decisions that are consistent with your known desires. You may, but are not required to, state your desires about the kinds of medical care you do or do not want to receive, including your desires concerning life support if you are seriously ill. If you do not want your agent to have the authority to make certain decisions, you must write a statement to that effect in the space provided below; otherwise, your agent will have the broad powers to make health care decisions for you that are outlined in paragraph 3 above. In either case, it is important that you discuss your health care desires with the person you appoint as your agent and with your doctor(s).

(Following is a general statement about withholding and removal of life-sustaining treatment. If the statement accurately reflects your desires, you may initial it. If you wish to add to it or to write your own statement instead, you may do so in the space provided.)

I do **not** want efforts made to prolong my life and I do **not** want life-sustaining treatment to be provided or continued: (1) if I am in an irreversible coma or persistent vegetative state; or (2) if I am terminally ill and the use of life-sustaining procedures would serve only to artificially delay the moment of my death; or (3) under any other circumstances where the burdens of the treatment outweigh the expected benefits. In making decisions about life-sustaining treatment under provision (3) above, I want my agent to consider the relief of suffering and the quality of my life, as well as the extent of the possible prolongation of my life.

If this statement reflects your desires, initial here: _____

Other or additional statements of medical treatment desires and limitations: <u>Provisions (1),(2),and (3)</u>
_____<u>above include the use of food.</u>_____
_____
_____
_____

(You may attach additional pages if you need more space to complete your statements. Each additional page must be dated and signed at the same time you date and sign this document.)

5. APPOINTMENT OF ALTERNATE AGENTS (OPTIONAL)

(You may appoint alternate agents to make health care decisions for you in case the person you appointed in Paragraph 2 is unable or unwilling to do so.)

If the person named as my agent in Paragraph 2 is not available or willing to make health care decisions for me as authorized in this document, I appoint the following persons to do so, listed in the order they should be asked:

First Alternate Agent: Name <u>Scott Alan Jones</u>   Work Telephone (_____) _____ _____

Address _____<u>1234 Oak, Folsom, Ca 95689</u>   Home Telephone (<u>XXX</u>) <u>XXX-XXXX</u>

Second Alternate Agent: Name <u>Anne Louise Riley</u>   Work Telephone (_____) _____

Address _____<u>1234 5th, Sacramento, Ca 95825</u>   Home Telephone (<u>XXX</u>) <u>XXX-XXXX</u>

6. USE OF COPIES

I hereby authorize that photocopies of this document can be relied upon by my agent and others as though they were originals.

2

HOME SWEET WELL MANAGED HOME

DATE AND SIGNATURE OF PRINCIPAL

6-11

(You must date and sign this power of attorney)

I sign my name to this Durable Power of Attorney for Health Care at __Fair Oaks_____, __CA__

(City)   (State)

on _____ (Fill in the date and then sign) _____

(Date)   (Signature of Principal)

STATEMENT OF WITNESSES

(This power of attorney will not be valid for making health care decisions unless it is either (1) signed by two qualified adult witnesses who personally know you (or to whom you present evidence of your identity) and who are present when you sign or acknowledge your signature or (2) acknowledged before a notary public in (*) If you elect to use witnesses rather than a notary public, the law provides that none of the following may be used as witnesses: (1) the persons you have appointed as your agent and alternate agents; (2) your health care provider or an employee of your health care provider; or (3) an operator or employee of an operator of a community care facility or residential care facility for the elderly. Additionally, at least one of the witnesses cannot be related to you by blood, marriage or adoption, or be named in your will. IF YOU ARE A PATIENT IN A SKILLED NURSING FACILITY, YOU MUST HAVE A PATIENT ADVOCATE OR OMBUDSMAN SIGN BOTH THE STATEMENT OF WITNESSES BELOW AND THE DECLARATION ON THE FOLLOWING PAGE.)

I declare under penalty of perjury under the laws of (*) that the person who signed or acknowledged this document is personally known to me to be the principal, or that the identity of the principal was proved to me by convincing evidence;* that the principal signed or acknowledged this durable power of attorney in my presence, that the principal appears to be of sound mind and under no duress, fraud, or undue influence; that I am not the person appointed as attorney in fact by this document; and that I am not the principal's health care provider, an employee of the principal's health care provider, the operator of a community care facility or a residential care facility for the elderly, nor an employee of an operator of a community care facility or residential care facility for the elderly.

(Have two witnesses sign and complete this section)

Signature _____   Signature _____

Print name _____   Print name _____

Date _____   Date _____

Residence Address _____   Residence Address_____

_____   _____

(AT LEAST ONE OF THE ABOVE WITNESSES MUST ALSO SIGN THE FOLLOWING DECLARATION)

I further declare under penalty of perjury under the laws of (*) that I am not related to the principal by blood, marriage, or adoption, and, to the best of my knowledge I am not entitled to any part of the estate of the principal upon the death of the principal under a will now existing or by operation of law.

Signature:_____ (Have one witness sign) _____

---

*The law allows one or more of the following forms of identification as convincing evidence of identity: a (*) driver's license or identification card or U.S. passport that is current or has been issued within five years, or any of the following if the document is current or has been issued within five years, contains a photograph and description of the person named on it, is signed by the person, and bears a serial or other identifying number: a foreign passport that has been stamped by the U.S. Immigration and Naturalization Service: a driver's license issued by another state or by an authorized Canadian or Mexican agency; or an identification card issued by another state or by any branch of the U.S. armed forces. If the principal is a patient in a skilled nursing facility, a patient advocate or ombudsman may rely on the representations of family members or the administrator or staff of the facility as convincing evidence of identity if the patient advocate or ombudsman believes that the representations provide a reasonable basis for determining the identity of the principal.

* Enter Name of State   3

6-72

SPECIAL REQUIREMENT: STATEMENT OF PATIENT ADVOCATE OR OMBUDSMAN

(If you are a patient in a skilled nursing facility, a patient advocate or ombudsman must sign the Statement of Witnesses above __and__ must also sign the following declaration.)

I further declare under penalty of perjury under the laws of (*)_____ that I am a patient advocate or ombudsman as designated by the State Department of Aging and am serving as a witness as required by subdivision (f) of Civil Code Section 2432.

Signature: _____   Address: _____

Print Name: _____   _____

Date: _____   _____

CERTIFICATE OF ACKNOWLEDGMENT OF NOTARY PUBLIC

(Acknowledgment before a notary public is __not__ required if you have elected to have two qualified witnesses sign above. If you are a patient in a skilled nursing facility, you __must__ have a patient advocate or ombudsman sign the Statement of Witnesses on page 3 __and__ the Statement of Patient Advocate or Ombudsman above)

(Have notary public complete and sign this section)

)

)ss.

County of _____)

On this _____ day of _____, in the year _____,

before me, _____,

(*here insert name and title of the officer*)

personally appeared _____

(*here insert name of principal*)

personally known to me (or proved to me on the basis of satisfactory evidence) to be the person whose name is subscribed to this instrument, and acknowledged to me that he or she executed the same in his or her authorized capacity, and that by his or her signature on the instrument the person executed the instrument.

WITNESS my hand and official seal.

_____

(*Signature of Notary Public*)

NOTARY SEAL

COPIES

YOUR AGENT MAY NEED THIS DOCUMENT IMMEDIATELY IN CASE OF AN EMERGENCY. YOU SHOULD KEEP THE COMPLETED ORIGINAL AND GIVE PHOTOCOPIES OF THE COMPLETED ORIGINAL TO (1) YOUR AGENT AND ALTERNATE AGENTS, (2) YOUR PERSONAL PHYSICIAN, AND (3) MEMBERS OF YOUR FAMILY AND ANY OTHER PERSONS WHO MIGHT BE CALLED IN THE EVENT OF A MEDICAL EMERGENCY. THE LAW PERMITS THAT PHOTOCOPIES OF THE COMPLETED DOCUMENT CAN BE RELIED UPON AS THOUGH THEY WERE ORIGINALS.

* Enter name of State   4

TRUSTEE INSTRUCTIONS
Managing Your Revocable Living Trust

The "trustee" is responsible for managing the trust assets. As the trustee of your own Revocable Living Trust, your responsibilities for managing your assets do not differ significantly. You are the owner of your assets, whether the assets are in your trust or not, and you can control, sell or borrow against your property just as you always could.

You should always strive to keep careful records of all transactions that affect your Revocable Living Trust; however there is no need for special accounting records or tax return forms.

Especially important are the actions you take to designate what assets you wish directed to your identified individual beneficiaries. You may have requested that certain percentages of your estate should be passed on to specified individuals or members of your family. However, your Trust Minutes can be utilized to make specific bequests as well. For example, you may have indicated that your estate should be divided equally ("share and share alike") among your children at your death. You can use your Trust Minutes to pass specific assets of your trust to individual children.

Broad powers are given to you as trustee, but you should always exercise prudence in managing your assets. Your Revocable Living Trust is your basic estate plan which will provide the foundation for a well organized estate.

YOUR TRUST ESTATE

As trustee, you hold your assets in trust for your own benefit during your life. When you place assets in your trust, you should identify those assets as belonging to "The (your name) Family Trust, (your name) Trustee". This simply means that your trust owns the asset and you own the trust.

To transfer real property to your trust, simply utilize a "quit claim deed" which can easily be recorded with your county recording office or other local government entity. Personal property, such as bank accounts, automobiles, etc., can be transferred by contracting the office or bank where the asset is recorded or held. Each bank, publicly traded corporation, or motor vehicle department has its own procedure for recording titles. In most instances, only a letter is required for changes of title. Of course, some assets are not titled or recorded. Simply list the description of such assets in your Schedule of Trust Assets.

TRUST MINUTES

Just as companies hold meetings and take specific actions which are recorded through the use of "Minutes," you can take specific actions affecting your trust through the use of your Trust Minutes. As suggested above, you may wish to use your Trust Minutes to designate the disposition of specific assets after your death. Major modifications of your trust should be accomplished through formal amendments. Many of the minor actions you wish to take can be accomplished through your Trust Minutes.

Think of your Trust Minutes as directions to your successor trustee. These directions can help your successor trustee in distributing your estate according to your specific wishes.

Example 6-5[5*]

Trust Schedule "D"
Jim and Sue Living Trust Gifts
Beneficiary: Son John

2002		Amount
02-16-02	Cash, help with auto repairs	$ 400
04-03-02	Check, help with income tax due	$ 700
08-20-02	Cash, for dental work	$ 350
120-01-02	Check, annual gifting	$5,000
	2002 TOTAL	$6,450

2003		Amount
06-04-03	Cash, for vacation trip	$ 600
09-02-03	Check, for quarterly income tax	$ 300
12-01-03	Check, annual gifting	$6,000
	2003 TOTAL	$6,900

---

[5] * Pages 6-76 and 6-77

Example 6-5

Trust Schedule "D"
Jim and Sue Living Trust Loan
Beneficiary: Daughter Mary

Loan for remodeling of kitchen, $9,000 on June 2, 2002

Check Date	Repayment Amount	Loan Balance
07-01-02	$400	$8,600
08-03-02	$500	$8,100
09-02-02	$600	$7,500
10-01-02	$500	$7,000
11-04-02	$400	$6,600
12-01-02	$600	$6,000
12-25-02	$-0-	$-0-

Balance of loan forgiven in lieu of annual gifting.

Trust Gifts
Beneficiary: Daughter Mary

2002		Amount
04-03-02	Check, for income tax due	$ 500
12-25-02	Forgive loan balance	$6,000
	2002 TOTAL	$6,500

2003		Amount
12-01-03	Check, annual gifting	$6,000

SUMMARY

By deciding to avoid probate - the costly and time consuming process of court supervised administration of your estate - you have taken an important step not only for you but for your family as well.

Like anything else, a Revocable Living Trust can appear to be very complicated. However, it is not.

Just remember, you are managing the assets of your trust. When you transfer your home or other assets to your trust, you control everything. You can "revoke" your trust at any time. You never risk your property by creating a Revocable Living Trust.

CHAPTER 7

ESSENTIALS OF TIME LINE PLANNING

THE TIME LINE
TIME LINE PLANNING
APPOINTMENT CALENDAR
FAMILY EVENTS DIARY

ESSENTIALS OF TIME LINE PLANNING

The Time Line

The earth travels one orbit around the sun in a segment of time designated as one year (to do this in 365¼ days the earth must race along the 584,000,000 mile orbit at 66,600 miles per hour!). This basic segment of time is divided into calendar months and weeks based on days the length of which is derived from the time required for the earth to rotate once on its axis. Days, of course, are divided into anti and post meridian periods, hours, minutes, and seconds. The constant and relentless progress through these segments of time may be thought of as the time line. Time is of the essence because once a period of it has been spent it is not capable of being repeated.

Time Line Planning

There is a unity between the time line and the planning and performing of activities. Many successful people make activity planning a part of their everyday life so that a reasonable relationship may be maintained between reaching objectives and the expenditure of time. For the purposes of this book, planning is divided into three categories: long term; intermediate term; and short term. Of course, planning may be made for any future period of time and for one or for all aspects of your life. Generally, rather broad categories of objectives are included in long term planning while more specific objectives are included in short term planning.

Planning requires that you make choices. Your choices have gotten you wherever you are right now and your choices will determine where you will be in the future. Choices that are the best for you and incorporated into a written time line plan give you a series of objectives to which to strive. With a plan, good decisions are made more frequently than they are without a plan and success is much more likely.

A long-term plan might include the following types of information:

Plan Number	Plan Dates	Objective
1.	2006-2010	Graduate from high school.
2.	2010-2014	Graduate from college with a B.S. in mechanical engineering.
3.	2014	Find employment in engineering.

4.	2014-2015	Marry college sweetheart.
5.	2016	Buy a house. Start a family.
6.	2017	Start a college education fund for your child and start other investments for yourself.

Plan Number	Plan
1.	Maintain a high grade point average not only to learn the subject matter but also to earn scholarships for college. Take college preparation courses with emphasis on science and mathematics. Participate in a school sport and student government activities.
2.	Enroll in a college with a good engineering reputation. Pay for the estimated cost of $80,000 from these sources:

Education fund set up by parents	$30,000
Scholarships	10,000
Part time work, summers	10,000
Government student loan	30,000
TOTAL	$80,000

Maintain a high grade point average. Participate in at least one school activity. Work only during summer vacations. Find "the" special girl.

Plan Number	Plan
3.	Start looking for employment well ahead of graduation date. Be persistent until engineering-type employment is found. Over a period of three or four years, work at several different types of engineering jobs and then select the type that is preferred for the long haul; if required, change companies during this three or four year period. For long term employment go to work for a large company.
4.	Marry "the" special college sweetheart.
5.	Buy a house with the savings started two years ago. Start a family.
6.	If a child comes along, start a college education fund under the Unified Gift to Minors Act. Start growth-type investments for retirement purposes.

An intermediate term plan might include the following types of information (for perhaps a forty-year old person):

Plan Number	Plan Dates	Objective
1.	2006	Buy a new auto.
2.	2007	Continue service work in a church.
3.	2007-2008	Learn more about investing for retirement.
4.	2006-2010	Plan for annual vacation trips.
5.	2006-2010	Develop closer ties with parents and grandparents.

HOME SWEET WELL MANAGED HOME

Plan Number	Plan
1.	Decide the sources of funds with which to buy a new auto. Study auto features, value ratings, and dealer costs. Select an auto and negotiate the price.
2.	Determine where services are most needed and volunteer for that work. Prefer adult ministry.
3.	Study strategies for investing in stocks, bonds, mutual funds, IRA's, 401K's, commodities, etc. Rather than rely on brokers, make all my own investment decisions to attain retirement and other financial objectives.
4.	Decide on probable destinations for vacation trips for each of the next five years. Estimate the cost of each trip and regularly set aside money to pay for each of these trips.
5.	Arrange for spending more time together for meals, fun outings, and other activities. Determine special needs of parents and grandparents and, if possible, do something about them.

A short term plan might include the following types of information:

Plan Number	Plan Date	Objective
1.	Today	In order of priority, perform tasks a, b, and c at work.
2.	Today	Have lunch with spouse.
3.	Today	Service auto.
4.	Today	Spend quality time with son.
5.	Today	Watch news on T.V.
6.	Today	Spend quality time with spouse.

Plan Number	Plan
1.	Arrive at work at least thirty minutes before scheduled start time to collect data and materials for task a, b, and c. Be sure to complete these tasks on time and before the end of the day.
2.	Have lunch with spouse and discuss mutual interests and activities.
3.	At a service center, have oil changed, have auto lubricated and have tire pressure and all engine fluid levels checked.
4.	Play ball with son, review his school activities and home work. Help him with his homework by giving him guidance.
5.	Watch one national and one local T.V. broadcast.
6.	Discuss the day's activities, plans for tomorrow, and play a game of cards.

While it is essential to write down long and intermediate term plans it probably isn't necessary to write down daily plans – unless you had a complicated life. However, many very successful and famous people do make a daily written plan, one that is reviewed at the end of the day followed by the writing of a plan for the next day.

Before arising in the morning, allow a few minutes to plan your objectives and priorities for the day including those pertaining to your health, your work, your family, your interpersonal relationships, your hobby, your service work, etc. It only takes a few minutes and it pays big dividends.

The plans described above are abbreviated ones with only enough information included to present a planning concept. Real time planning would include more specific details and probably many more objectives.

Whenever you have a choice, which you almost always have, spend only the amount of time performing a task that the value of the task warrants. To spend time on a useless task is a complete waste. For efficiency, think enough about each task ahead of time to perform it correctly the first time it's done.

To be sure, good time line planning greatly improves the chances of making wise choices and decisions and of attaining many objectives in a timely manner. It also contributes to building confidence, satisfaction, and a feeling of accomplishment. It is a far better alternative than one in which you are guided by the whims of the moment.

Appointment Calendar

It is essential to use an appointment calendar. A spiral bound monthly calendar or a weekly appointment book is acceptable. In the appropriate date space record the appointment time, the person with whom you are to meet (or the event), and-unless obvious – the appointment location.

Family Events Diary

While not essential, sometimes the recording of family history events – births, marriages, special gatherings, awards, graduations, deaths, out of town trips, household moves, etc. – is invaluable. Probably on a weekly or monthly basis, record the description of the event, the date/s, and any pertinent observations.

CHAPTER 8

ESSENTIALS OF A COLLEGE EDUCATION FUND

ESTIMATE OF COLLEGE COSTS
SET AN AFFORDABLE SAVINGS/INVESTMENT GOAL
DEVELOP AN INVESTMENT PLAN
GET STARTED WITH YOUR SAVINGS PLAN
RESPONSIBILITIES OF THE STUDENT
EDUCATION FUND DISBURSEMENT PLAN

ESSENTIALS OF A COLLEGE EDUCATION FUND

Investing for a child's college education is one of the most important investments a parent, grandparent, or custodian will ever make because the benefit implications for the child are endless. Even though a college education is very expensive, especially if you have more than one child, with a well thought out plan implemented very early in a child's life, adequate funds for this purpose can usually be obtained. For most families there are several sources from which to obtain all of the money required to cover college education costs including amounts provided by parents, grandparents, scholarships, grants, and loans.

For that part of college education money to be provided by parents and grandparents a plan including the following six steps is essential:

1. Prepare detailed estimate of college costs.
2. Set an affordable savings/investment goal.
3. Develop an investment plan to meet the savings goal.
4. Get started with your savings plan.
5. Define the responsibilities of the student.
6. Develop an education fund disbursement plan.

Estimate of College Costs

This estimate should be based on a college plan that will most likely be followed by the child. Consider whether or not the child will live at home for all or part of his college years. Will the student most likely attend a junior college then finish in a senior college, or go only to a senior college? What is the preferred college? What is the anticipated level of degree to be obtained – bachelors, masters, doctors, other? What is the planned number of years to be spent attending college?

The cost estimate for a student that plans to live at home, attend a junior college for two years, and then attend a senior college for two years would include the following types of expenses:

Junior College

Auto (if needed)	$10,000
60 units at $30 per unit	1,800
Books and supplies, 20 classes at $50 each	1,000
Student fees of $300 per semesters x4	1,200
Living expenses & insurance, $300 per month x21	6,300
Subtotal	$20,300

<u>Senior College</u>

60 units at $400 per unit	$24,000
Book and supplies, 20 classes at $75 each	1,500
Student fees at $500 per semester x4	2,000
Living expenses & insurance, $300 per month x21	<u>6,300</u>
Subtotal	$33,800
Total	$54,100

The cost of attending a well known private school for four years and living away from home could be $100,000 or more.

What the price of a college education will be in ten or fifteen years cannot be accurately predicted. However, it is helpful for planning purposes to make a ballpark estimate and then to set an affordable savings goal.

Set An Affordable Savings/Investment Goal

As a part of your regular household budget and after plans are in place to provide for ordinary household and retirement expenses, budget a fixed amount that you can set aside on a regular basis for a college education fund. Aim for at least 50% of estimated college costs.

The compounding effect of regular investments can, over time, be significant. For example, starting at the birth of a child and continuing for seventeen years, a $100 a month investment compounded at an annual rate of 6.0% would yield a total of approximately $35,000. This amount could be a significant part of the total amount needed to cover college education costs. Based on the above estimate of $54,100 and the investment formula of $100 a month, the sources of all required monies might include the following:

Education fund	$35,000
Scholarships and grants	5,000
Student summer-work earnings	3,000
Federal student loans	<u>11,100</u>
TOTAL	$54,100

Since they are gifts, scholarships and grants do not need to be repaid. They are usually given based on outstanding athletic or academic merit or on financial need. Usually these awards cover less than ten per cent of total college costs.

There are work-study programs available but these are not recommended because it is preferred that a student spend as much time as possible on studies and school activities. However, summer work with little or no studying is recommended.

The best way to ensure that college education monies will be available is to set up and consistently contribute to a personal savings/investment fund. Any amount you are able to contribute toward education costs will lighten the burden of repaying student loans. The sooner you start the less you will have to contribute because the money will have longer to earn compounding interest.

Develop An Investment Plan

To meet a planned education fund goal there are several investment options from which to choose: Uniform Gifts/Transfers to Minors Act (UGMA/UTMA) accounts, 529 college savings plans, 529 prepaid tuition plans, U.S. savings bonds, tax-managed funds, tax-exempt bonds – federal and state municipal bonds, and other options. Only the UGMA/UTMA – type investment plan is addressed in this text because it provides some income tax advantages while permitting complete control of investments by the account custodian. Since it requires the managing of investments by the custodian, this type of plan may not be right for every family.

A UGMA/UTMA plan is one in which a named custodian, usually a parent, sets up and manages an investment account owned by the beneficiary child. The invested money is registered in such an account under the child's Social Security number and is taxed accordingly. There is an income tax advantage since the child's tax obligation is almost always less than that of the custodians. The custodian determines the specific investment to be made, adds monies to this investment account, changes investment plans when necessary, and eventually withdraws money from the education fund for use by the college student. After an affordable savings goal has been established and an investment plan has been developed then it's time to get started.

Get Started With Your Savings Plan

Whichever plan you select or goal you set, it is essential to start at the earliest possible time. Starting within the first month or two after a child is born is not too early. It is also essential to stick to your savings plan faithfully. The sooner you start, the less money you'll have to put away because your assets will have more time to grow.

With a goal and plan in mind, select the best investment medium you know of, determine its requirements, fill out an application for an account, and send in the first investment amount. A very good place to start is with a successful and well established mutual fund such as The Vanguard Group in one of its many productive stock growth funds. This group offers most of the major college education fund investment options including the 529 plan.

A contribution of $100 per month compounded at an annual rate of 6.0% would yield the following approximate amounts:

Year	Cumulative Total	Year	Cumulative Total
1	$1,200	10	$16,300
2	2,500	11	18,500
3	3,900	12	20,800
4	5,400	13	23,300
5	7,000	14	26,000
6	8,600	15	28,800
7	10,400	16	31,800
8	12,200	17	34,900
9	14,200		

Responsibilities of the Student

Just before the student starts high school the custodian should fully explain to him or her the provisions of the in-place college education fund plan. This information should encourage the student to make good grades to earn scholarships, and should make it easier for all concerned to plan on sources of money to cover all estimated college costs.

Just before actually starting college, an agreement should be developed between the custodian and student covering the latter's responsibilities to be met in return for receiving college fund monies. This agreement, in written form, will differ with each family and set of circumstances but could include such things as the following:

1. The student attends college on a full-time basis earning enough credits to graduate with a primary degree in not more than five years.
2. The student does not use any illegal street drugs and does not abuse the use of alcohol.
3. The student has decided, without reservation, the college major and minor subjects to be taken.
4. The student maintains a grade point average equivalent to a "B" average.
5. Before each school year begins and in a timely manner, the student provides the custodian with a list of subjects to be taken, the related number of credits, and the estimated costs of tuition, books and supplies, and student fees for the entire school year (no plan, then no money is to be provided).
6. The student provides the custodian with a copy of the grade report immediately after the completion of each semester.
7. The student will spend all fund monies only for planned education purposes.
8. The student is to participate in at least one extracurricular activity during all years of college.

Education Fund Disbursement Plan

Once a student's college plans have been made, it is then essential to craft a disbursement plan that best fits his, or her, needs. A description of one tried and proven plan covering several options is included in the following table.

Annual Payout Per Cent of Accrued Fund Balance

Year	Option "A"	Option "B"	Option "C"	Option "D"
1	18	25	12	20
2	22	33	14	25
3	50	50	16	32
4	100	100	50	50
5	--	--	100	100

Accrued fund balance is the balance at the beginning of each <u>school</u> year. Option definitions are as follows:

Option "A":	Two years at a two-year junior college, followed by two years at a senior college.
Option "B":	Four years at a senior college.
Option "C":	Two years at a two-year junior college, followed by three years at a senior college.
Option "D":	Five years at a senior college.

Payments, interest earned, and balances based on these pay out per cents, and a hypothetical starting amount of $20,000, are shown in the following table.

HOME SWEET WELL MANAGED HOME

Payment, Interest, Balance
(Interest, 6.0% per year)

Description	Option "A"	Option "B"	Option "C"	Option "D"
Start Balance	$20,000	$20,000	$20,000	$20,000
First Year Payment	-3,600(18%)	-5,000(25%)	-2,400(12%)	-4,000(20%)
Balance	16,400	15,000	17,600	16,000
Interest Earned	+1,000	+900	+1,100	+1,000
Balance	17,400	15,900	18,700	17,000
Second Year Payment	-3,800(22%)	-5,300(33%)	-2,600(14%)	-4,200(25%)
Balance	13,600	10,600	16,100	12,800
Interest Earned	+800	+600	+1,000	+800
Balance	14,400	11,200	17,100	13,600
Third Year Payment	-7,200(50%)	-5,600(50%)	-2,700(16%)	4,400(32%)
Balance	7,200	5,600	14,400	9,200
Interest Earned	+400	+300	+900	+600
Balance	7,600	5,900	15,300	9,800
Fourth Year Payment	-7,600(100%)	-5,900(100%)	-7,650(50%)	-4,900(50%)
Balance	-0-	-0-	7,650	4,900
Interest Earned	-	-	+450	+300
Balance	-	-	8,100	5,200
Fifth Year Payment	-	-	-8,100(100%)	-5,200(100%)
Ending Balance	-	-	-0-	-0-

Priorities for the use of fund distributions are: (1) tuition; (2) books, supplies and student fees; and (3) monthly living expenses. In Option "A" above, assuming a cost of $900.00 for tuition and books for the first year (paid to the student at registration time before each semester), then the balance of the $3,600.00, i.e. $2,700.00 would be paid to the student at a rate of $300.00 per month for the months of September through the following May ($2,700 divided by 9 = $300 per month).

Other options for the distribution of fund monies might include the following:

1. If the student decides to attend a trade school or a vocational school rather than a regular academic college, payment of fund monies will be made as needed for such schooling, including living expenses, as agreed to by the fund custodian/trustee and the student.
2. Any money remaining in the fund after the student graduates from college or from a trade school shall be paid to him, or her, on the twenty-second birthday anniversary of the graduate.

The key to successful college financing is to give a child's education enough of a priority to prepare a workable, affordable contribution plan, to start contributing to it as early as possible, and to faithfully build a fund until the time it's needed. Wonderful rewards to all concerned can be realized if you develop and follow a realistic roadmap to reach your college savings goals within the allowable time frame.

CHAPTER 9

ESSENTIALS OF GOOD HEALTH

EXERCISE
NUTRITION
DRINKING WATER
AIR QUALITY
CLEANLINESS
SLEEP
WORK ENVIRONMENT
MEDICAL AND DENTAL CARE
WEIGHT CONTROL
STRESS MANAGEMENT

ESSENTIALS OF GOOD HEALTH

The Basis of Good Health

Several factors contribute to good health including the genes you inherited, the amount of exercise you get, nutrition, the water you drink, the air you breathe, cleanliness, proper sleep, your work environment, medical and dental care, how you control your weight, and how you handle stress.

Exercise

Other than the genes you inherited, adequate exercise is probably the single most important requirement for maintaining good physical and mental health. Get moderate exercise every day, sixty minutes or more in not more than two sessions. Exercise regardless of your age. Give exercise a very high priority. Exercise early in the day and again an hour after the last meal of the day. Exercise in two basic ways – aerobic and weight resistance. To avoid injury, exercise well within your capabilities. For example, a fast two-mile walk probably gives you as much benefit as jogging or running two miles. One very good low impact exercise is rowing on a high quality rowing machine. To make rowing less boring, position your machine so that you can watch television while you row. In this way a twenty to thirty minute rowing session seems to pass very quickly. There are other low impact exercise machines that will provide equal benefits. Swimming is probably the optimum exercise. However, there is a risk involved when you swim in chlorinated water.

A natural adjunct to physical activity is stretching. It improves your flexibility and helps prevent tight, stiff muscles. When you stretch, include your calf, thigh, hips and low back muscles, and your neck and shoulders. Each stretching movement should be done slowly and held for ten to thirty seconds.

There is considerable data demonstrating the value of staying physically active. These include helping: to reduce the risk of premature death, particularly from cardiovascular disease; to prevent weight gain and its related problems; to build and maintain healthy muscles, bones, and joints; to maintain strength and good balance; to reduce the risk of high blood pressure; to reduce the risk of developing dementia, diabetes and cancer; and to promote psychological well-being including reductions in stress, depression, and anxiety. In addition to these important benefits, adequate exercise makes you feel physically and mentally more alive than if you don't exercise. With all these life giving benefits you simply cannot fail to exercise on a daily basis.

If there is any uncertainty about it, check with your doctor to develop a plan that suits your situation. This is especially important if you have been inactive for a long period of time.

Nutrition

To attain vibrant health and a long life, a nutritious food plan is an absolute essential. From time to time our food needs and desires change because of varying activity levels, seasonal changes, stress levels, our age, and many other factors. Nevertheless, there are general guidelines to follow that include essential food groups. These groups are listed below in decreasing order of food value, quantity to be consumed, and importance for good health. More foods in Group One should be eaten than foods in Group Two and more foods should be eaten in Group Two than in Group Three, etc. Most food pyramids and other guidelines specify numbers of servings to be consumed in each food group. This rarely works because how many of us measure and count servings? The recommended foods and food groups, listed in descending order of importance, are as follows:

Group 1

Foods high in valuable nutrition such as vegetables, fruits, whole grains such as rice and oats, bran cereals, and unrefined whole-grain breads. Stand back and take a good look at a well-stocked produce department of a supermarket. Of the dozens and dozens of vegetable and fruit items, think about how many of these you eat on a regular basis. Is it ten or perhaps twenty percent? To maintain your vital capacity at a high level, it would make an amazing difference to increase this number to perhaps eighty or ninety percent. Furthermore, it makes good sense to eat these foods as raw as possible since cooking them in any way destroys some or all of their nutrients.

Group 2

High quality protein including fish, skinless chicken, skinless turkey, natural lean red meats, eggs, low fat milk products, and legumes.

Group 3

Cheeses, nuts, seeds, olive oil and other natural oils and spices.

Group 4

General application food supplements – vitamins, minerals, herbs, amino acids, enzymes – made from natural foods in whole or concentrated forms. Specific application supplements such as antioxidants and those for the cardiovascular system, joints, colon, prostate, brain, etc.

Group 5

Sugar, partially hydrogenated oils, salt, food preservatives and other chemicals, and processed carbohydrates. Avoid these items as much as possible. Altogether they are the largest known preventable cause of ill health and degenerative diseases in this country.

Breakfast is a very important meal. The following is one that is packed with nutrition and requires about five minutes to prepare:

1. Fruit smoothie (serves three)
    Mix in a blender:
    1 banana
    1 cup fresh blueberries
    8 oz. low fat blueberry yogurt
    1 cup non fat milk and 1 cup 1% milk
    2 rounded tbls. good quality whey protein powder
    1 rounded tbls. low potency vitamin, mineral, amino supplement in powder form.

Flavors other than blueberries may be used – strawberries and strawberry yogurt, apricots and vanilla yogurt, peaches and peach yogurt, etc.

2. Whole grain bread, toasted and spread with a small quantity of peanut butter.
3. Hot, caffeine free herbal tea such as mint, licorice spice, spearmint, apple cinnamon, chamomile, orange, etc.

Drinking Water

Regardless of the quality of the tap water in your household a good filter for your drinking water is an essential protective investment. Under-the-sink stainless steel filter and a separate drinking water faucet are recommended. The filters used should be able to screen out taste and odor, chlorine, chloramine, lead, mercury, trihalomethanes, chlordane, VOCs, dichloroethane, PCBs, toxophene, MTBEs, particulate matter, asbestos, cysts and turbidity. Filters should be changed regularly and well before they approach their rated capacity. A filter should be replaced when the unit's rated capacity or rated time period approaches, when the flow rate slows, or when the filter becomes saturated with bad tastes or odors. They should be certified by NSF international to reduce a wide range of contaminants of health concern.

How much water should you drink? Because of widely differing conditions, it is difficult to answer this question in terms of a specific quantity. One answer that fits most conditions is this: besides satisfying your natural thirst, drink enough water to keep your urine almost clear. When you do this you know that you are drinking enough water.

HOME SWEET WELL MANAGED HOME

Air Quality

It is important for good health to breathe clean air at all times. To live in an environment filled with contaminated air, especially smog, gives you a good chance of developing some kind of pulmonary disease, including lung cancer, and could shorten your life by up to five years. Cigarette smoking is by far the most common cause of pulmonary disease especially primary lung cancer. Other causes of pulmonary system diseases are: air pollution, including so-called passive second-hand smoke, traffic fumes, and smokestack emissions; exposure to toxic substances such as radon, carbon monoxide, and radioactive gases, asbestos, and arsenic; chronic bronchitis, and bacterial and fungal infections.

To prevent pulmonary diseases, don't smoke and severely limit your exposure to second-hand smoke. If at all possible move out of a city that has entrapped polluted air – Los Angeles, Sacramento, Phoenix, etc. – and live and work where the air is clean. Homes may be tested and monitored for radon and carbon monoxide by using devices available in most hardware stores. Periodic chest x-rays and computed tomography and magnetic resonance imaging scans are highly recommended, especially in high-risk areas. If possible, avoid strenuous activities in contaminated air.

Cleanliness

Of course an essential part of good health is cleanliness. It pays big dividends to keep both mind and body clean. As for the mind, think about whatever is true, whatever is noble, whatever is right, whatever is pure, whatever is lovely, whatever is admirable, whatever is excellent or praiseworthy and whatever is productive. Do not think about those things that are evil or that are a waste of time. Contributing significantly to optimum health is a clean body, both internally and externally. It is well worth the effort to keep yourself clean along with your clothing and possessions. Avoid any contamination that you think might be harmful.

According to the Centers for Disease Control and Prevention, alcohol-based gels, rinses, or foams offer several advantages when used as an adjunct to washing the hands with soap. Alcohol-based hand rubs damage structural components of bacteria, various fungi, and some viruses on contact, unlike soap and water which merely loosens and rinses away microorganisms and debris. It has been demonstrated that alcohol-based hand rubs are as much as 1,000 times more efficient at eliminating harmful bacteria, fungi, and viruses from hands.

Sleep

It is a basic essential that you get enough sleep to get through your day without getting drowsy. One of the keys in reaching this goal is to go to bed at approximately the same time each night so you can set your system's circadian rhythm, the "body clock" that regulates most internal functions. It is equally important to arise at the same time each morning. Self discipline is required to learn and maintain good sleep habits.

Don't sleep "in" trying to make up for lost sleep – that goes for weekends as well. Schedule your meals so that you don't go to bed within three hours of eating. Don't exercise within an hour of going to bed. Rather, set aside some quiet time to reflect on the day's activities or to play some low-excitement game. Use your bedroom only for sleep and sex. Don't watch T.V., read, eat, talk on the phone, have serious discussions with anyone, or perform mundane tasks in bed.

Create a comfortable sleep setting. Make your bedroom as comfortable as possible. Give a very high priority to the purchase of a good mattress and box spring or other bed of choice. Soundproof the room and hang curtains that keep out the light. Assure that the bedroom temperature is just right – not too cold, not too hot. Use a small, silent clock. Keep electric clocks and clock radios at least four feet distance from any part of your body.

Avoid stimulants such as caffeine for at least eight hours before you retire. Do not drink an alcoholic nightcap. Don't drink a lot of fluids before bed, especially if you're older; you might wake up later in the night for a bathroom call. If you take medication at bed time make certain that it doesn't have the effect of stimulants. If necessary, use mechanical aids such as earplugs, eyeshades, or electric blankets. Learn and practice muscle relaxation techniques and program yourself to reduce the volume of thoughts going through your mind.

Work Environment

So much time is spent at work that it is essential that you do whatever is necessary to work in a safe and healthy environment. If special equipment is required for protection from heat, cold, vapors, particles, chemicals, etc., be sure to use such protection. Key factors for office-type work include proper lighting, chairs designed for back support, comfortable working level desks and tables, non-glare computer monitors, and circulating fresh air (as opposed to recirculated air). In any work, it is essential to manage your circumstances to keep stress levels as low as possible. Allow adequate time for a nutritious breakfast and an unhurried trip to work. Take time to plan your work day and to set priorities. Whenever possible, complete one task before you start the next one. Minimum use should be made of stimulants such as coffee and depressants such as alcohol.

Medical and Dental Care

Make good use of all of the various types of medical care available to you including conventional medical doctors, complementary and alternative medical doctors, chiropractors, internet services, and publications of highly rated medical institutions (Mayo Clinic, Johns Hopkins, etc.). The team approach to medical care usually produces the best results.

It certainly pays dividends to get all required immunizations, at any age, and to get required periodic physical examinations. It is far better to make a concerted effort to prevent diseases then it is to try to cure them. When medical treatment is required and if there is any question about the diagnosis, do not hesitate to obtain a second or even third opinion.

For almost everyone, some form of health insurance protection is required for good health care provided on a timely basis.

Keep on hand a good up-to-date book on prescription drugs such as the Johns Hopkins Complete Home Encyclopedia of Drugs. This type of book is invaluable and includes brand names, principal uses, dosages, side effects, onset of effect, duration of action, dietary advice, storage requirements, instructions for discontinuing use, effects of prolonged use, precautions, drug, food, and alcohol interactions, and other special factors. The information in this type of book should be studied before taking any prescription drug.

When faced with any affliction that needs to be treated, obtain and study any available information that is applicable so that you will be prepared to help your care giver make informed decisions. A good source of such information is the complete home medical reference book <u>Symptoms and Remedies</u> by Johns Hopkins. There are other similar books including those that include descriptions of complementary medicine remedies. It is very important to do your own thinking and to watch out for your own interests.

Maintain a health diary and keep one for each family member. For each medical and dental event, record the date, name of the care giver, the diagnosis, the treatment used, and any required future actions.

Obtain and file a copy of all medical reports applicable to you and your children including blood, x-ray, imaging, and operative reports. Study these reports and follow-up on any further evaluation or action needed.

For medical information, set up and maintain a separate file and file container. Include therein your medical diary, medical reports, and health insurance information. Set up a separate file folder for each medical care giver and in each one file the applicable medical data.

Proper dental care begins at home with good oral hygiene practices particularly brushing of the teeth within ten minutes after eating. To avoid an excessive buildup of hardened plaque (tartar) and calculus have your teeth professionally cleaned at regular intervals – sometimes as often as bi-monthly. Sometimes, once a year is adequate. Professional dental care is needed to prevent gingivitis (inflammation of the gums) and the more serious periodontitis. Vitamin supplements may be needed to treat a nutritional deficiency. Periodic x-rays of the mouth and repair of teeth are obvious essentials of good dental care. Corrective dentistry of children's teeth should be done at the optimum age established for each procedure.

Weight Control

There are several essential factors to be considered in any weight control program. Of course, the basic concept is to use up more calories than you consume from the food you eat. For most people, including children, weight control is a life-long problem. In the long run a healthy lifestyle, even though difficult, is much better than short programs of dieting. The key to weight control is a combination of adequate exercise and making the right food choices.

An exercise regimen as previously described in this chapter is an absolute requirement. It is very difficult to control or lose weight if you live a sedentary life style. An exercise program must be developed and followed on a regular day after day basis.

A reasonable food plan is also described earlier in this chapter. It's important to choose a variety of foods and it's unnecessary to boycott a food or food group entirely. Portion size control works better than eliminating foods. For example, you should allow yourself small amounts of sweets, processed carbohydrates, and fats. Never eat until you feel stuffed full.

When you eat is almost as important in a weight control program as the type of food you eat. The English have an applicable saying that goes like this: "Eat the breakfast of a king, the lunch of a queen, and a dinner of a pauper." Another very helpful rule to follow is to never eat between meals. Late evening snacks are decidedly a no-no. Sometimes, especially for older retired people, a two-meal-a-day eating schedule, like 9:00AM and 4:00PM, works well in controlling weight.

If you drink alcoholic beverages, there are two good rules to follow: never have more than one drink per day; never have a drink and eat dessert during the same day. A drink mix of citrus, tomato, or fruit juice contains fewer calories than a sweet carbonated one.

If your weight is at an acceptable level, set a minimum-maximum weight range of four pounds. When your weight edges up to the maximum of the range, lose three or four pounds – which is not too difficult to do. To lose a larger amount is quite difficult.

Achieving your health and weight goals requires a great deal of constant motivation and dedication. But if you are successful you'll look better and feel better too.

Stress Management

Stress is the tension you feel when faced with a new, unpleasant or threatening situation. In response to stress a change occurs in a person's normal behavior because it throws the body out of balance by overloading one or more of its mechanisms. At times this can be a good thing as in weight training to build muscles since the body responds by building an increased capacity. So long as this type of stress is only moderate and involves only mechanisms that are designed to improve, then stress can be beneficial. Unfortunately most of the stress we experience is either too much or presents our body with things it does not know how to manage. This type of stress decreases our vitality and weakens our health.

Stress management essentials include the addressing of methods of controlling factors that require a response or change within a person by identifying the stressful situation, eliminating the negative stressors, and then developing effective coping mechanisms to counteract the response in a constructive manner. You can learn to manage your stress so that you feel calm instead of nervous, in control instead of hassled, at peace instead of angry, refreshed and renewed instead of frazzled, and alive instead of burned out.

Plan a personal stress management program. Exercise on a daily basis is essential. Prefer an activity that requires all of your concentration such as golf, tennis, or bowling. Full concentration on an activity pushes the rest of the world into the background. Games that require concentration such as bridge and cribbage have the same effect. Manage your time so that you are not rushing through meals or to appointments or to work. Setting aside time for yourself for exercise, recreation, and relaxation is important for good health. If you do these stress-reducing activities regularly and with commitment you will notice the benefits immediately.

If your schedule of activities is overloaded, drop some of the activities and learn to say "no." When you do this, be sure to consider important priorities such as your health, your family, your work, your church and service work, etc.

Hobbies you really enjoy can also reduce stress. Other practices that should be a part of your stress reduction program include getting enough sleep, eating right, managing your time wisely, taking breaks, breathing deeply, talking out your problems with a trusted friend, and even practicing meditation. Don't accept harmful substitutes such as alcohol, caffeine, nicotine, or tranquilizers for your stress management. Barbiturates and tranquilizers should be taken only if prescribed by your doctor, and even then they should not be continued for to long periods of time because of adverse side effects.

Only you can make the lifestyle changes that bit by bit will enable you to reduce the stress in your life and maintain vital mental and physical health.

The choices we make concerning good health affect every facet of our lives. Good health practices are not negotiable nor can they be done on a hit-or-miss basis if we are to realize our optimum potential. It won't work to make good health choices "someday" or "tomorrow," it needs to be done "today" and "every day."

CHAPTER 10

ESSENTIALS OF HOUSE AND AUTO MAINTENANCE

House Maintenance
Equipment Replacement and Remodeling
Auto Maintenance

ESSENTIALS OF HOUSE AND AUTO MAINTENANCE

House Maintenance

To operate efficiently, to make things around the house last longer, and to save money your home needs periodic checkups and basic maintenance care. All too often breakdowns occur at the worst possible time. These can be held to a minimum by developing and following a good maintenance program. Regular inspection of the following items, usually done on an annual basis, is an essential part of such a program:

Heating and air conditioning systems
Electrical system
Plumbing system, water softeners, water filters.
Toilet tanks and bowls and septic tank
Kitchen stove/oven and refrigerator
Dishwasher
Microwave oven (built-in)
Garbage disposal
Clothes washer and dryer
Water heater
Garage door and door opener
Ceiling and exhaust fans
Ductwork and exhausts
Exterior walls and foundation
Roofing
Gutters and downspouts
Doors and windows
Basement and crawlspace
Drainage around house perimeter
Outside faucets
Automatic sprinkler system
Areas paved with concrete, asphalt, or brick
Main gas and water shut-off valves
Electrical circuit box
Well and palatability and safety of well water

Fireplace and chimney

Inspections of major household appliances should include the items described in the <u>maintenance</u> section of the applicable operating instructions booklet. Other inspections that are essential include the following general categories:

Water and moisture damage; plumbing leaks; dripping faucets both inside and outside the house; leaking toilet tank valves; rain leaks on roof and around pipes, chimneys, windows, and doors; rain damage near the outlets of rain gutter downspouts; pools of water collecting along foundations and basements, patios and porches; crawl spaces; soil erosion from runoff of rain and melted snow; and water heater rust and leaks.

Rusted areas on any items and surface touched by moisture.

Rust colored water coming from water faucets.

Loose connections, covers and mounting brackets whether plumbing, electrical, or mechanical.

Paint failure – bare spots, cracking, peeling, blistering.

Dust, dirt, and lint accumulations in clothes dryer exhaust pipes, air conditioner compressors, refrigerator coils, ductwork, between furniture and walls, etc.

Loose nails and screws in roof, in rain gutters, in house siding, in fencing, and in other wood surfaces.

Check for missing, rotted, split or bowed roof shingles.

Infestation by termites or other pests – look for termite shelter tubes and small piles of wood dust.

Loose or missing caulking or putty – around bathtubs, wash basins, windows, flashing, etc.

Door locks, deadbolts, and door and window weather-stripping.

Cracking, eroding, root damage, or missing pieces of concrete, asphalt and brick surfaces.

Inspect all yard tools and machines for rust, dull cutting edges, and proper lubrication. At the start of winter check to make sure that gasoline is drained from all gasoline-powered machines.

Operating condition of pilot lights, thermostats, electrical circuit box switches, and circuit loads.

For winter, if freezing is expected, check insulation around outside water pipes and faucets.

Venting pipes and pipe connections for gas water heaters.

Many household inspection and maintenance jobs can be done by the homeowner. However, others such as those for the heating and air conditioning units should be done by a reliable licensed and insured contractor. Any problems found during the inspection process should be corrected in a timely manner. It is far easier to maintain and repair one or two items on a regular basis than it is to have to do many jobs at one time.

Equipment Replacement and Remodeling

Four essential tasks are required to replace major items of household equipment and to remodel a part of your house:

1. Prepare a detailed statement of work/specifications.
2. Obtain bids from at least three licensed and insured contractors.

3. Evaluate bids and award the contract.
4. Check the new equipment and monitor its installation or the remodeling work.

A typical statement of work/specifications for a major item such as replacement of heating and air conditioning equipment would include such things as the following: Trane gas furnace model TUC60, upright, 56,000 BTUs, 92% AFU efficiency; Trane air conditioner model TTP036, 3-ton, 35,000 BTUs, 13 SEER, evaporative coil model HA1036; White-Rodgers digital temperature control box model F8024; suction and liquid lines, freon, new vent pipe and cap, new condensate drain, new condenser pad, vibration isolation pads, new gas line and valve, new electrical pig tail and whip connector, low-voltage wiring; new cold air return duct; inspect all air ducts and seal all air duct leaks; new 16" x 25" electrostatic air filter; and haul away all replaced equipment and scrap materials.

A statement of work/specifications for remodeling a bathroom might include such items as the following: new Kohler Villager tub; new Farmington standard lavatory with a 1.6 gallon water-saver tank; Delta Model DR5 single control faucet; number 1125 Mexican Sand tile 5 feet above tub on three sides, around window, counter top, and 1 foot above counter top on two sides; shower head to be 70 inches above floor; new Miami-Carey triple door mirrored bathroom cabinet; new oak cabinet to fit vanity area; three new oak towel racks each 30 inches long and new oak paper holder/magazine rack; new GE Model GB095 two-bulb light fixture installed on center 8 inches above bathroom cabinet; new 4-inch mercury shower vent and fan unit centered over middle of tub with new wall switch; repaint walls, ceiling, and doors with paint furnished by owner; replace linoleum floor covering with Armstrong Style G1172 linoleum; and haul away all replaced equipment and scrap materials.

If necessary, obtain the assistance of the bidding contractors to develop a mutually satisfactory statement of work and schedule for the job. Specify a start date, the number of consecutive days, and a completion date. Payment terms should also be included.

Following the completion of the statement of work, obtain three bids and evaluate them on the basis of experience of the contractor, your confidence in him, his references, a review of some of his work done for others, and the bid price. It should be recognized that the lowest bidder is not necessarily the best one for you.

After the contract is signed the work should be carefully monitored to make certain that the specified items are being installed and that the statement of work is being followed exactly. Unless absolutely necessary do not make any in-process changes since they are usually very expensive. Final payment should not be made until a final inspection has been done and the work completed to your satisfaction.

Auto Maintenance

To get the most out of your auto at the lowest cost requires an adequate maintenance and repair program. Performing the inspections and procedures specified in your owners manual is required to comply with the terms of the warranties covering your vehicle. These procedures must be performed at the specified intervals to assure that your warranty remains in effect. Based on the requirements set forth in the owners manual an efficient and easy way to do this is to prepare a mileage or interval schedule in the formats shown below. These schedules should be recorded in a 3" x 5" bound notebook kept in the glove compartment for easy reference. It should be made when you first acquire a vehicle and every 20,000 miles thereafter.

Mileage Schedule and Procedure:
(LOFF means lube, oil change, new oil filter, and check engine and transmission fluid levels)

1,000	LOFF, change from break-in to regular oil.
4,000	LOFF
7,000	LOFF; rotate tires
10,000	LOFF
12,000	Replace air cleaner filter; inspect brake hoses, lines, pads, calipers, and rotors; inspect exhaust pipe and muffler; inspect suspension mounting bolts; inspect steering gear box, linkage, and arm ball joints; check air conditioning refrigerant; align wheels.
13,000	LOFF
14,000	Rotate tires
16,000	LOFF
19,000	LOFF

Under severe driving conditions these procedures should be done more frequently.

Interval Schedule and Procedure:

If an auto isn't driven enough to use a mileage schedule, then an interval schedule should be followed.

Assume an auto purchase date of July 1, 2004

Check air pressure in tires at least every two weeks.

October 1, 2004	LOFF, change from break-in to regular oil.
April 1, 2005	LOFF
October 1, 2005	LOFF
April 1, 2006	LOFF; replace air cleaner filter, inspect brake hoses, lines, pads, calipers, and rotors; inspect exhaust pipe and muffler; inspect suspension mounting bolts; inspect steering gear box, linkage, and arm ball joints; check air conditioning refrigerant.
October 1, 2006	LOFF, rotate tires; align wheels

When any maintenance or repair work is done to your auto the following should be recorded in the same 3" x 5" notebook in which the schedule is recorded; odometer reading, date, description of work done, name of service agency, and cost.

A good maintenance program for your house and auto requires time, effort, and money, but it pays big dividends in maintaining value, reliability, safety, appearance, and long-term cost savings. For work performed, the bids, contracts, receipts, warranties, operating instructions, parts lists, etc., should be filed in the applicable asset file.

CHAPTER 11

ESSENTIALS OF INVESTING

Identify Your Options
List of Priorities
Investment Budget Plan
Rule of 72
Table of Compounding Interest
Master Investment Record

ESSENTIALS OF INVESTING

The key to successful investing is to identify your options, develop an inclusive list of priorities, and then prepare and follow a budget plan to reach your investment objectives.

Identify Your Options

Investment options will vary for each family or individual situation depending on the total income available and the desired end objectives. A limited income might provide for only the basic living expenses. On the other hand, a high income might provide for a wide array of investments. Whatever the income, it pays to consider each option before deciding which is best for you. For this purpose, a list of meaningful priorities needs to be carefully developed.

List of Priorities

After basic living expenses have been covered, the following investment objectives, listed in order of priority, might be considered as typical for many families or individuals:

1. Purchase living quarters––house, condo, mobile home.
2. Cover your insurance needs––health, disability, property and casualty life, etc.
3. Set aside money for a "rainy day" fund to be used as a financial emergency reserve. It is generally recommended that you put enough into this fund to cover your basic expenses for six months. This investment reserve should be one that is quickly available––a no load mutual fund, a money market account, a certificate of deposit, treasury bills, etc.
4. Establish retirement plans such as 401Ks and IRAs.
5. Establish children's education funds––UGMA/UTMA accounts, 529 college savings plans, 529 prepaid tuition plans, U.S. savings bonds, tax-exempt bonds, etc.
6. Invest in mutual funds, individual stocks, and bonds.
7. Trade in commodity futures and options.

HOME SWEET WELL MANAGED HOME

Investment Budget Plan

It is essential to develop and follow a household budget of cash, expenses, and income as described in Chapter Three of this book. You must carefully budget household cash and expenses, compare them to spendable income, and then invest any balance in ways that enable you to build financial security.

In the development of a good investment plan, several factors should be considered including the following:

1. Set realistic goals and use self discipline to strive to attain them. You must fight the tendency to assume that the future will take care of itself.
2. Become informed about how to get your money to work for you effectively. Learn how to avoid investment pitfalls.
3. Except for buying your house, stay out of debt. Excessive and uncontrolled debt is devastating to personal wealth and your financial future.
4. Since they consume money and wealth, avoid making poor investments. If an investment sounds too good to be true, it probably is.
5. The tax burden is a major drain on the dollars you earn, so steps should be taken to lighten this burden whenever possible through the use of deferred and tax-exempt investments.
6. Be sure to consider the effects of inflation––it eats away the purchasing power of your money so you must continually plan to overcome its effects.

The following calculations show the net return after taxes and inflation. These calculations are based on an investment of $1,000, earnings of 10% interest, an inflation rate of 4%, and a tax bracket of 28%.

A.	Investment Amount	$1,000
B.	Interest Earned (10%)	100
C.	Total A and B	$1,100
D.	Less Tax on Income (.28 x $100)	-28
E.	Net After Taxes (C – D)	$1,072
F.	Less Inflation (.04 x $1,072)	-43
G.	Net After Taxes and Inflation	$1,029
H.	Net Return (G – A ÷ A)	2.9%

It is obvious that tax-deferred and tax-free investments should play an important part of your long term savings strategy. There's not much you can do about the effects of inflation so it's important to remember that the cost of food, clothing, medical treatment, autos, and entertainment do not go down upon retirement. In fact, they will probably go up. When planning for retirement, keep these costs in mind.

7. Do not procrastinate getting started and following a sound investment plan. Time is your ally when used wisely and your enemy when it is not.

8. Calculate your net worth each year and track it consistently. Add up your total assets (the value of the equity in your home, your retirement accounts, stocks, bonds, mutual funds, personal property and cash). Then subtract your total liabilities (unpaid mortgage balance, auto loan balance, credit card and department store debt, unpaid personal loan amount, etc.). In the long run you want to see your net worth moving steadily upward.

9. Keep in mind a helpful planning tool called the "Rule of 72." Simply stated, divide 72 by your interest rate to determine the number of years required to double your money. At 6.0% interest it would take twelve years to double your money (72 ÷ 6); at 8.0% it would take nine years. The same formula can be used for any interest rate.

10. During your working years, select investments that provide compounding earnings wherein dividends, interest, and capital gains are automatically reinvested. It's the concept of making "interest-on-interest."

Table of Compounding Interest
<u>Annual Investment of $1,000</u>

<u>Number of Years</u>	<u>Annual Rate of Return and Cumulative Total Amount</u>		
	<u>6%</u>	<u>8%</u>	<u>10%</u>
5	$5,980	$6,340	$6,720
10	13,980	15,650	17,530
15	24,670	29,320	34,950
20	38,990	49,420	63,000
25	58,160	78,950	108,180
30	83,800	122,350	180,940
35	118,120	186,100	298,130
40	164,050	279,780	486,850

Of course these totals are pre-tax amounts. It's surprising how much a savings of about $85 a month can yield over time.

11. In investing it is necessary for you to periodically determine the risk-reward position with which you are comfortable. The general rule is: the lower the risk, the lower the yield and, conversely, the higher the risk, the higher the yield. Commodity futures and options trading is a very high risk investment whereas insurance and savings are the most secure.

Risk evaluation and investment timing are closely related. The first and cardinal rule of timing: regardless of the type of investment, "buy at a low price and sell at a high one." Timing for the long haul is also very necessary and at least three different time periods should be considered.

A. Up to the age of fifty, a 90% stock and 10% bond investment allocation is reasonable since there would be time to wait for a stock market recovery. One of the best places to put your money is in an index-type mutual fund covering a wide market of growth and aggressive growth stocks. With such a fund, investment professionals manage your money and broad diversification is realized.

B. From Age 50 until retirement, a 50% stock and 50% bond allocation might yield enough earnings to reach a reasonable retirement goal. If not, a higher stock allocation may be necessary.

C. At retirement the investment allocation should change to 90% bonds and 10% stocks. The objectives are to protect the capital amount, to provide a steady income, and––with stocks–– to provide a hedge against inflation.

It should also be recognized that switching from taxable to tax-free investments will increase the amount of spendable, after-tax income while reducing the dollar amount of money subject to taxation, and might reduce the rate at which your income is taxed. Also, if such a switch succeeds in reducing your tax bracket, Social Security pension benefits would be taxed at a lower federal tax rate.

It is essential that the investment plan, the budgeted amounts, the allocation mix, and the asset diversification are tailored specifically for each family's or individual's financial objectives, time horizon, and tolerance for risk. Research has shown that investors who have savings goals are twice as likely to save enough as those who don't set goals.

Master Investment Record

Record the purchase and sale of each investment made in stocks, bonds, mutual funds, real estate, etc. For mutual funds and other investments where frequent purchase and redemptions are made, record only the initial purchase and final redemption information. Exclude those investments for which periodic reports will be received automatically (retirement 401's, periodic purchases and redemptions of mutual fund shares, education 529's, day-trading transaction reports, etc.)

The information to be recorded in the Example 11-1 form is adequate for the purposes of a master investment record. An entry should be made immediately following the acquisition of each investment asset and, subsequently, immediately following the sale of each asset. The source of the money used to acquire each investment should be recorded as well as the disposition of proceeds realized at the time each asset is sold. This information provides a traceability record of investment buying and selling monies and a record that will become invaluable to the trustees of a living trust or will.

Each page of this record should be numbered sequentially and filed in the investment section of the asset file.

National® Brand 45-606 Eye-Ease®
45-306 2-Pack
Made in USA

		Initials	Date
NAME: Jim and Sue		Prepared By	
MASTER INVESTMENT RECORD		Approved By	

Example 11-1

PAGE

NO.	INVESTMENTS
1.	Description: Common stock, Gencorp, 100 shares
	Date Purchased & Broker Name: June 6, 2000, Prudential Financial (Ron Jones)
	Total Amount Paid & Source of Funds: $2,050 from savings account.
	Where Applicable, Interest Rate & Maturity Date: (NA)
	Date Sold, Sale Price, & Use of Proceeds: October 1, 2003, net $3,000. Used for
	purchase of Item No. 2 bonds.
2.	Description: Bonds, Lodi, Calif. Project 2004-3, two $5,000 bonds
	Date Purchased & Broker Name: October 8, 2003, M.L. Stern & Co. (Robert Smith)
	Total Amount Paid & Source of Funds: $10,000 Item 1 stock sale & savings account.
	Where Applicable Interest Rate & Maturity Date: 5.75% interest, matures 10/8/15
	Date Sold, Sale Price & Use of Proceeds:
3.	Description: Mutual fund shares, Primecap Fund, 20 shares
	Date Purchased & Broker Name: November 18, 2003, The Vanguard Group
	Total Amount Paid & Source of Funds: $950, from savings account.
	Where Applicable Interest Rate & Maturity Date: (NA)
	Date Sold, Sale Price & Use of Proceeds:
	Description:
	Date Purchased & Broker Name:
	Total Amount Paid & Source of Funds:
	Where Applicable Interest Rate & Maturity Date:
	Date Sold, Sale Price & Use of Proceeds:
	Description:
	Date Purchased & Broker Name:
	Total Amount Paid & Source of Funds:
	Where Applicable Interest Rate & Maturity Date:
	Date Sold, Sale Price & Use of Proceeds:

CHAPTER 12

ESSENTIALS OF A PERSONAL NATURE

PERSONAL AREAS OF RESPONSIBILITY AND RESPECT
ESSENTIALS OF CARING FOR PET DOGS AND CATS
ESSENTIALS OF AN EVERLASTING LIFE

ESSENTIALS OF A PERSONAL NATURE

Personal Area of Responsibility

When trying to do a task not attempted before by himself, have you heard a very young child say "no, Mommie, I can do it"? In effect, such a child is following a necessary and natural tendency to enlarge his area of responsibility. This practice continues with an ever increasing frequency as the child gets older. Inevitably, responsibility is learned and assumed for a wide range of tasks – eating, walking, dressing, bathing, cleaning teeth, playing more advanced games, doing household chores, riding bicycles, using ever more complex household equipment, studying, etc. By the late teens the child's responsibility world has, or should have, grown to a very large size. By age eighteen most children believe they can manage most any responsibility without much, if any, help.

This same process of enlarging a person's area of responsibility – that is, in performing tasks without anyone else's help – should continue throughout one's life until the frailty of old age stops it. It is essential to recognize that when someone has taken on the responsibility for doing some task, either by assignment or by assuming it, he should be allowed to do it without any directions or interference by anyone else. This is a cardinal rule that should be followed by everyone, especially among family members. Of course, if the responsible person asks for directions or help or if there is an unrecognized physical danger or a chance for great embarrassment, then directions or assistance should be volunteered. This interference should occur only rarely.

Uninvited directions or assistance is actually an insult to the intelligence of the person doing the task. Such intrusions cause disharmony, anger, bickering, inefficiencies, and other negative effects. If continued, it is very destructive to interpersonal relationships.

There is a companion cardinal rule to follow by the person doing the task. In a kind way, this person should not allow anyone to interfere by issuing unwanted directions or giving unwanted assistance unless, of course, he requests it.

An example of how easy it is to break these cardinal rules can be demonstrated by describing what could happen between a married couple going to a market together. With the husband assuming the responsibility for driving, his wife, on the way out the door says, "Don't forget the keys and be sure to lock the door." Again, a short time later at the market parking lot with many empty parking spaces available, she points and says, "there is a good place to park." Within a short period of time, the wife – probably thinking that she is being helpful – has invaded her husband's area of responsibility and has insulted his intelligence three times. In effect, she has made his responsibility world smaller. The husband, of course, should not allow this to happen because if this interference becomes a common occurrence, then his responsibility world will actually become smaller – with all sorts of negative results.

The responsibility for doing a particular task might change from one person at one time to someone else the next time. This is a common occurrence within a family setting wherein many household chores have to be done. Regardless of who is doing the task, the above two cardinal rules should be followed. Sometimes it might be necessary to have a discussion and then reach an agreement about who actually has the responsibility. Also, at times, more than one person will work on a task at the same time. Even in this situation there should be an agreement about who does each part of the task. Of course, when someone is giving or receiving instructions about how to do a new task, then the above rules for area of responsibility do not apply.

In addition to an area of responsibility, each person has an area of respect. The same philosophy applies here also in that this area for one person should not be invaded by anyone else unless it is to prevent an injury or a great embarrassment. This is especially needed in the relationships between husband and wife and between parents and their children. Regardless of the old adage that "respect has to be earned," everyone's area of respect should be carefully honored.

The cardinal rules of areas of responsibility and respect are derived from the golden rule: "in everything, do unto others as you would have them do unto you."

Essentials of Caring for Pet Dogs and Cats

The decision to acquire a dog or cat should be made only after careful consideration is given to the long-term care that such a pet requires. While children can provide some help, only an adult should assume the responsibility for caring for pets. Essential requirements for taking care of dogs and cats include the following:

1. From a veterinarian or pet store, buy a book on how to take proper care of the particular breed of pet you have acquired. Carefully follow the instructions set forth in this book.
2. Food is very important to your pet. Use a variety of both meat and kibble flavors on a rotation basis. Feed pets twice a day in an amount that is not too much or too little. It pays to feed them high quality foods. Feed them table scraps only infrequently.
3. Make sure your pets have clean drinking water at all times – filtered water is best. Use stainless steel or glass water dishes rather than one made of plastic. Do not use a hose to fill water dishes because it adds a disagreeable taste to the water. Fill dishes only from faucets. Clean water dishes often.
4. Pets need lots of companionship, both the human kind and with other pets of the same breed and gender. It makes a world of difference to have two dogs or two cats, and it is essential if no one is home during the work day.
5. Since they love to run, daily running exercise for dogs is imperative. For this, an open field is best, but other types of exercise will do – such as the use of a leash with an adult jogger. If a bicycle is used with a dog on a leash, great care must be taken not to cause over exertion of the dog. Many dogs die from this type of over exertion, especially in warm weather.
6. Make certain that your pet receives all required immunizations. It is much less expensive to prevent diseases than it is to cure them.
7. As soon as it's old enough, have your pet neutered.
8. If you must use a litter box for your cats, clean and deodorize it as soon as possible after each use.

9. During cool or cold weather provide a warm place for your pets. If necessary, use an enclosure heated by 500 watt electric lamps. During hot weather provide a cool place for them.

10. Beds and bedding for pets should be soft, smooth, and clean. Never allow pets to sleep on a bare floor, especially a concrete one. Cats prefer to sleep in a bed that is elevated a foot or two above the floor.

11. Prevent your pets from getting into fights with other dogs or cats, and do whatever it takes to prevent them from attacking a human. If your pet is injured in a fight or sustains any injury, take it to a veterinarian as soon a possible. If you delay and the wound becomes infected then the care becomes very expensive or the pet may expire.

12. Keep your dogs clean, brushed, and groomed. Keep your cats brushed, perhaps twice a week, and give them Petro Malt or a similar hair-ball control supplement. When they need plaque buildup removed, have your pets teeth professionally cleaned.

13. When your pet has a painful, incurable disease – such as cancer – or when it is in constant pain from old age, then be kind and have it painlessly put to sleep.

    To properly care for a pet takes a lot of time, energy and money. However, the enjoyment and returned affection make it all worthwhile.

Essentials of an Everlasting Life

To realize the fullest possible measure of love, joy, peace of mind, contentment, freedom, and success, you must "get right" with your Creator God by learning about Him, by praying to Him, by worshiping Him in church, by following His laws about how to live, by giving Him of your time, talents, and money, by telling others about Him, and by believing in the authority and saving grace of His son Jesus Christ.

Laws and instructions on how to live the best possible life are found in the Holy Bible. Some of the most essential and most familiar of these, arranged in random order, are as follows (New International Version):

1. <u>God Loves Us – The Gospel Message</u>
    Now, brothers and sisters, I want to remind you of the gospel I preached to you, which you received and on which you have taken your stand. By this gospel you are saved, if you hold firmly to the word I preached to you. Otherwise, you have believed in vain.
    For what I received I passed on to you as of first importance: that Christ died for our sins according to the Scriptures, that he was buried, that he was raised on the third day according to the Scriptures. Corinthians 15:1-4

2. <u>The Holy Bible</u>
    All scripture is God-breathed and is useful for teaching, rebuking, correcting and training in righteousness, so that the man of God may be thoroughly equipped for every good work. 2 Timothy 3:16

3. The Golden Rule

    So in everything, do to others what you would have them do to you, for this sums up the law and the Prophets. Matthew 7:12

4. Creation of the Earth and the Heavens

    In the beginning God created the heaven and the earth. Genesis 1:1

5. The Seventh Day, Saturday, The Sabbath

    By the Seventh day God had finished the work he had been doing; so on the seventh day he rested from all his work. And God blessed the seventh day and made it holy, because on it he rested from all the work of creating that he had done. Genesis 2:2 & 3

    When the Sabbath was over – very early on the first day of the week, just after sunrise, they were on their way to the tomb – Matthew 16:1 & 2

    NOTE: The first day of the week is Sunday; the seventh day, Saturday, is the Sabbath.

6. The Ten Commandments

    You shall have no other gods before me.

    You shall not make for yourself an idol in the form of anything in heaven above of on the earth beneath or in the waters below. You shall not bow down to them or worship them; for I, the Lord your God, am a jealous God, punishing the children for the sin of the fathers to the third and fourth generation of those who hate me, but showing love to a thousand generations of those who love me and keep my commandments.

    You shall not misuse the name of the Lord your God, for the Lord will not hold anyone guiltless who missuses his name.

    Remember the Sabbath day by keeping it holy. Six days you shall labor and do all your work, but the Seventh day is a Sabbath to the Lord your God. On it you shall not do any work, neither you, nor your son or daughter, nor your manservant or maidservant, nor your animals, nor the alien within your gates. For in six days the Lord made the heavens and the earth, the sea, and all that is in them, but he rested on the seventh day. Therefore the Lord blessed the Sabbath day and made it holy.

    Honor your father and your mother, so that you may live long in the land the Lord your God is giving you.

    You shall not murder.

    You shall not commit adultery.

    You shall not steal.

    You shall not give false testimony against your neighbor.

    You shall not covet your neighbor's house. You shall not covet your neighbor's wife, or his manservant or maidservant, his ox or donkey, or anything that belongs to your neighbor. Exodus 20:3-17.

7. The Beatitudes

    Blessed are the poor in spirit, for theirs is the kingdom of heaven.

    Blessed are those who mourn, for they will be comforted.

    Blessed are the meek, for they will inherit the earth.

Blessed are those who hunger and thirst for righteousness, for they will be filled.

Blessed are the merciful, for they will be shown mercy.

Blessed are the pure in heart, for they will see God.

Blessed are the peacemakers, for they will be called sons of God.

Blessed are those who are persecuted because of righteousness, for theirs is the kingdom of heaven.

Blessed are you when people insult you, persecute you and falsely say all kinds of evil against you because of me. Rejoice and be glad, because great is your reward in heaven, for in the same way they persecuted the prophets who were before you. John 5:1-12.

8. Love

Love is patient, love is kind. It does not envy, it does not boast, it is not proud. It is not rude, it is not self-seeking, it is not easily angered, it keeps no record of wrongs. Love does not delight in evil but rejoices with the truth. It always protects, always trusts, always hopes, always perseveres. I Corinthians 13:4-7.

9. The Two Great Commandments

"Teacher, which is the greatest commandment in the law?" Jesus replied:

"Love the Lord your God with all your heart and with all your soul and with all your mind. This is the first and greatest commandment. And the second is like it: Love your neighbor as yourself. All the law and the Prophets hang on these two commandments." Matthew 22:36-40.

10. The Work of God

Then they asked him, "What must we do to do the works God requires?" Jesus answered, "The work of God is this: to believe in the one he has sent." John 6:28 & 29.

11. The Shepherd Psalm

The Lord is my shepherd, I shall not be in want. He makes me lie down in green pastures, he leads me beside quiet waters, he restores my soul. He guides me in the paths of righteousness for his name sake. Even though I walk through the valley of the shadow of death, I will fear no evil, for you are with me: your rod and your staff, they comfort me. You prepare a table before me in the presence of my enemies. You anoint my head with oil; my cup overflows. Surely goodness and love will follow me all the days of my life, and I will dwell in the house of the Lord forever. Psalm 23.

12. God's Definition of Sin

Everyone who sins breaks the law; in fact, sin is lawlessness. I John 3:4.

13. The Sin That God Cannot Forgive

And so I tell you, every sin and blasphemy will be forgiven men, but the blasphemy against the Spirit will not be forgiven. Anyone who speaks a word against the Son of Man will be forgiven, but anyone who speaks against the Holy Spirit will not be forgiven, either in this age or in the age to come. Matthew 12:31 & 32.

14. <u>Things The Lord Hates</u>
There are six things the Lord hates, seven that are detestable to him: haughty eyes, a lying tongue, hands that shed innocent blood, a heart that devises wicked schemes, feet that are quick to rush into evil, a false witness who pours out lies, and a man who stirs up dissension among brothers. Proverbs 6:16-19.

15. <u>Treasurers in Heaven vs. Love of Money</u>
For the love of money is a root of all kinds of evil. Some people, eager for money, have wandered from the faith and pierced themselves with many griefs. I Timothy 6:10.
Do not store up for yourselves treasures on earth … But store up for yourselves treasures in heaven … For where your treasure is, there your heart will be also. Matthew 6:19-21.
No one can serve two masters – you cannot serve both God and money. Matthew 6:24.

16. <u>Two are Better Than One</u>
Two are better than one, because they have a good return for their work: if one falls down, his friend can help him up. But pity the man who falls and has no one to help him up! Ecclesiastes 4:9.

17. <u>Feed Your Enemy</u>
If your enemy is hungry, give him food to eat; if he is thirsty, give him water to drink. In doing this, you will heap burning coals on his head and the Lord will reward you. Proverbs 25:21 & 22.

18. <u>A Grandparent's Crown</u>
Children's children are a crown to the aged, and parents are the pride of their children. Proverbs 17:6.

19. <u>A Good Name</u>
A good name is better than fine perfume, and the day of death better than the day of birth. Ecclesiastes 7:1.

20. <u>Extremes</u>
… The man who fears God will avoid all extremes. Ecclesiastes 7:18.

21. <u>Eating, Drinking, Smoking</u>
Why spend money on what is not bread, and your labor on what does not satisfy? Listen, listen to me, and eat what is good, and your soul will delight in the richest of fare. Isaiah 55:2.
So whether you eat or drink or whatever you do, do it all for the glory of God. I Corinthians 10:31.
Wine is a mocker and beer a brawler; whoever is led astray by them is not wise. Proverbs 20:1.
Nor thieves nor drunkards not slanderers nor swindlers will inherit the kingdom of God. I Corinthians 6:10.
Don't you know that you yourselves are God's temple and that God's Spirit lives in you? If anyone destroys God's temple, God will destroy him; for God's temple is sacred and you are that temple. I Corinthians 3:16 & 17.

22. <u>Holy Wedlock or Unholy Deadlock?</u>

Unless the Lord builds the house, its builders labor in vain. Psalm 127:1.

Above all, love each other deeply, because love covers over a multitude of sins. I Peter 4:8.

In your anger do not sin. Do not let the sun go down while you are still angry, and do not give the devil a foothold. Ephesians 4:26 & 27.

Be kind and compassionate to one another, forgiving each other, just as in Christ, God forgave you. Ephesians 4:32.

So they are no longer two, but one. Therefore what God has joined together, let man not separate. Matthew 19:6.

A gentle answer turns away wrath, but a harsh word stirs up anger. Proverbs 15:1.

Do you see a man wise in his own eyes? There is more hope for a fool than for him. Proverbs 26:12.

23. <u>Work</u>

… We were not idle when we were with you, nor did we eat anyone's food without paying for it. On the contrary, we worked night and day, laboring and toiling so that we would not be a burden to any of you. We did this, not because we do not have the right to such help, but in order to make ourselves a model for you to follow. For even when we were with you, we gave you this rule: "If a man will not work, he shall not eat." 2 Thessalonians 3:7-10.

Six days you shall labor and do all your work. Exodus 20:9.

One who is slack in his work is brother to one who destroys. Proverbs 18:9.

24. <u>Orderliness</u>

But everything shall be done in a fitting and orderly way. I Corinthians 14:40.

25. <u>Accepting Instruction</u>

Whoever gives heed to instruction prospers, and blessed is he who trusts in the Lord. Proverbs 16:20.

26. <u>Control the Temper</u>

Better a patient man than a warrior, a man who controls his temper than one who takes a city. Proverbs 16:32.

27. <u>A Time for Everything</u>

There is a time for everything, and a season for every activity under heaven: a time to be born and a time to die, a time to plant and a time to uproot, a time to kill and a time to heal, a time to tear down and a time to build, a time to weep and a time to laugh, a time to mourn and a time to dance, a time to scatter stones and a time to gather them, a time to embrace and a time to refrain, a time to search and a time to give up, a time to keep and a time to throw away, a time to tear and a time to mend, a time to be silent and a time to speak, a time to love and a time to hate, a time for war and a time for peace. Ecclesiastes 3:1-8.

28. <u>Baptism</u>

Whoever believes and is baptized will be saved, but whoever does not believe will be condemned. Mark 16:16.

One Lord, One Faith, One Baptism, one God and Father of all, who is over all and through all and in all. Ephesians 4:5 & 6.

And now what are you waiting for? Get up, be baptized and wash your sins away, calling on his name. Acts 22:16.

Jesus answered, "I tell you the truth, no one can enter the kingdom of God unless he is born of water and the Spirit." John 3:5.

29. <u>The Body, The Spirit, The Soul, Death</u>

The Lord God formed the man from the dust of the ground and breathed into his nostrils the breath of life, and the man became a living being. Genesis 2:7. As the body without the spirit is dead … James 2:26.

… as long as I have life within me, the breath of God in my nostrils … Job 27:3.

… and the dust returns to the ground it came from, and the spirit returns to God who gave it. Ecclesiastes 12:7.

The soul who sins is the one who will die … Ezekiel 18:20.

For the living know that they will die, but the dead know nothing … Their love, their hate and their jealousy have long since vanished; never again will they have a part in anything that happens under the sun. Ecclesiastes 9:5&6.

Jesus replied, "The people of this age marry and are given in marriage. But those who are considered worthy of taking part in that age and in the resurrection from the dead will neither marry nor be given in marriage, and they can no longer die; for they are like angels." Luke 20:34-36.

30. <u>Judging and Condemning Others: Forgiving</u>

Do not judge, and you will not be judged. Do not condemn, and you will not be condemned. Forgive, and you will be forgiven. Luke 6:37.

31. <u>Jesus Christ</u>

I and the Father are one. John 10:30.

… Anyone who has seen me has seen the Father … John 14:9.

Then Jesus declared, "I am the bread of life. He who comes to me will never go hungry, and he who believes in me will never be thirsty …" John 6:35.

When Jesus spoke again to the people, he said, "I am the light of the world. Whoever follows me will never walk in darkness, but will have the light of life." John 8:12.

I came from the Father and entered the world; now I am leaving the world and going back to the Father. John 16:28.

32. <u>Angels</u>

The two angels arrived in Sodom in the evening, and Lot was sitting in the gateway of the city. When he saw them, he got up to meet them and bowed down with his face to the ground. Genesis 19:1.

That night the angel of the Lord went out and put to death a hundred and eighty-five thousand men in the Assyrian Camp - - - 2 Kings 19:35.

My God sent his angel, and he shut the mouths of the lions … Daniel 6:22.

When they had gone, an angel of the Lord appeared to Joseph in a dream. "Get up," he said "take the child and his mother and escape to Egypt" … Matthew 2:13.

There was a violent earthquake, for an angel of the Lord came down from heaven and, going to the tomb, rolled back the stone and sat on it. His appearance was like lightning, and his clothes were white as snow - - - - the angel said to the women, "Do not be afraid, for I know that you are looking for Jesus, who was crucified. He is not here; he has risen, just as he said. Come and see the place where he lay. Then go quickly and tell his disciples: He has risen from the dead …" Matthew 28:2&3; 5&7.

33. Never Say "You Fool"

But I tell you that anyone who is angry with his brother will be subject to judgement … But anyone who says "you fool" will be in danger of the fire of hell. Matthew 5:22.

34. Yes and No Answers

Simply let your "yes" be "yes" and your "no," "no;" anything beyond this comes from the evil one. Matthew 5:37.

35. Good Medicine

A cheerful heart is good medicine, but a crushed spirit dries up the bones. Proverbs 17:22.

36. The Lord's Prayer

"This, then, is how you should pray: "Our Father in heaven, hallowed be your name, your kingdom come, your will be done on earth as it is in heaven. Give us today our daily bread. Forgive us our debts, as we also have forgiven our debtors. And lead us not into temptation, but deliver us from the evil one." Matthew 6:9-13.

37. The Gardener, The Vine, The Branches

"I am the true vine, and my Father is the gardener. He cuts off every branch in me that bears no fruit … No branch can bear fruit by itself; it must remain in the vine. Neither can you bear fruit unless you remain in me. I am the vine; you are the branches. If a man remains in me and I in him, he will bear much fruit; apart from me you can do nothing." John 15:1-5.

38. Don't Be Afraid

"Do not let your heart be troubled and do not be afraid." John 14:27.

39. Evangelism

Then Jesus came to them and said, "All authority in heaven and on earth has been given to me. Therefore go and make disciples of all nations, baptizing them in the name of the Father and of the Son and of the Holy Spirit, and teaching them to obey everything I have commanded you." Matthew 28:18-20.

40. Little Children and the Kingdom of Heaven

Jesus said, "Let the little children come to me, and do not hinder them, for the kingdom of Heaven belongs to such as these." Matthew 19:14.

41. <u>The Millennium – a Summary</u>

Events to Occur at The Beginning of the 1,000 years:

A. Devastating earthquake and hailstorm (Revelation 16:18-21; Revelation 6:14-17).
B. Second coming of Jesus for His saints (Matthew 24: 30&31).
C. Righteous dead raised to life (I Thessalonians 4:16&17).
D. Righteous given immortality (I Corinthians 15:51-55).
E. Righteous given bodies like Jesus (I John 3:2; Philippians 3:21).
F. All righteous caught up into the clouds (I Thessalonians 4:16&17).
G. Living wicked slain by the breath of the Lord's mouth (Isaiah 11:4).
H. Wicked in graves remain dead until the end of the 1,000 years (Revelation 20:5).
I. Jesus takes righteous to heaven (John 13:33, 36; 14:1-3).
J. Satan bound (Revelation 20:1-3).

Events and Conditions to Occur During the 1,000 years:

A. Earth in battered condition from huge hailstones and devastating earthquake (Revelation 16:18-21; 6:14-17).
B. Earth in total blackout/bottomless pit (Jeremiah 4:23, 28)
C. Satan and his angels forced to stay on earth/bound (Revelation 20:1-3).
D. Righteous in Heaven participating in the judgement (Revelation 20:4).
E. Wicked are all dead (Jeremiah 4:25; Isaiah 11:4).

Events to Occur At the Close of the 1,000 Years:

A. Third coming of Jesus with his saints (Zechariah 14:5).
B. Holy city settles on Mount of Olives (Zechariah 14:4, 10).
C. The Father, angels, and all of the righteous come with Jesus (Revelation 21:1-3; Matthew 25:31; Zechariah 14:5).
D. Wicked dead raised; Satan loosed (Revelation 20:5, 7).
E. Satan deceives entire world (Revelation 20:8).
F. Wicked surround the Holy City (Revelation 20:9).
G. Wicked destroyed by fire (Revelation 20:9).
H. New heavens and earth created (Isaiah 65:17; 2 Peter 3:13; Revelation 21:1).
I. God's people enjoy eternity with Christ on the new earth (Revelation 21:2-4).

42. <u>Salvation, Grace, From Death To Life, Born Again</u>
Admit Three Things:
  I am a sinner. "For all have sinned …" (Romans 3:23).
  I am doomed to die. "For the wages of sin is death …" (Romans 6:23).
  I cannot save myself. " …apart from me you can do nothing." (John 15:5).
Repent:
  "…But unless you repent, you too will perish." (Luke 13:3).
Believe Three Things:

He died for me. " …now crowned with glory and honor because he suffered death, so that by the Grace of God he might taste death for everyone." (Hebrews 2:9).

He forgives me. "If we confess our sins, he is faithful and just and will forgive us our sins …" (I John 1:9).

He saves me. "I tell you the truth, he who believes has everlasting life." (John 6:47). "You should not be surprised at my saying, 'You must be born again.'" (John 3:7).

43. The Antichrist

There are at least nine characteristics of Antichrist described in the Bible:

The "little horn came up among them." (Daniel 7:8).

It would have a man at its head that would speak for it. (Daniel 7:8).

It would pluck up or uproot three kingdoms. (Daniel 7:8).

It would be diverse or different from the other ten kingdoms. (Daniel 7:24).

It would make war with and persecute the saints. (Daniel 7:21, 25).

It would emerge from the pagan Roman empire – the fourth world kingdom. (Daniel 7:7, 8).

God's people would be given into his hand for "a time and times and the dividing of time." (Daniel 7:25).

It would speak great words against God. (Daniel 7:25 and Revelation 13:5).

It would think to change times and laws. (Daniel 7:25).

44. The Holy Spirit

All that belongs to the Father is mine, that is why I said the Spirit will take from what is mine and make it known to you. John 16:15.

But the fruit of the Spirit is love, joy, peace, patience, kindness, goodness, faithfulness, gentleness and self-control. Against such things there is no law. Galatians 5:22 & 23.

But you will receive power when the Holy Spirit comes on you ----. Acts 1:8.

Don't you know that you yourselves are God's temple and that God's Spirit lives in you? I Corinthians 3:16.

Those who live according to the sinful nature have their minds set on what that nature desires; but those who live in accordance with the Spirit have their minds set on what the Spirit desires. The mind of sinful man is death, but the mind controlled by the Spirit is life and peace ---. Romans 8:5&6.

The Spirit himself testifies with our spirit that we are God's children. Romans 8:16.

45. The Conclusion of It All

Now all has been heard; here is the conclusion of the matter: Fear God and keep his commandments, for this is the whole duty of man. For God will bring every deed into judgement, including every hidden thing, whether it is good or evil." (Ecclesiastes 12:13&14).

In everything:
Do the best that you can do
Look the best that you can look
Be the best that you can be

CHAPTER 13

ESSENTIALS HOUSEHOLD MANAGEMENT FORMS

BUDGET OF CASH, EXPENSES, AND INCOME
ACTUAL EXPENSE PAYMENTS – RECURRING AND VARIABLE
ACTUAL EXPENSE PAYMENTS – MEDICAL, DENTAL, AND MISCELLANEOUS
CALCULATION OF HOUSEHOLD FINANCIAL POSITION
ESTIMATED SPENDABLE INCOME
POWER OF ATTORNEY FOR HEALTH CARE DECISIONS
MASTER INVESTMENT RECORD

To make copies of these forms it is recommended that you first cut them out of this book.

National Brand 45-606 Eye-Ease
45-306 2·Pack
Made in USA

	Initials	Date
NAME:	YEAR:	Prepared By
BUDGET OF CASH, EXPENSES, AND INCOME		Approved By

	BUDGET ITEM	(✓) JAN	(✓) FEB	(✓) MAR	(✓) APR	(✓) MAY	(✓) JUNE
1	1. Cash – 1st Half						
2	Cash – 2nd Half						
3	2. Recurring Expenses:						
4							
5							
6							
7							
8							
9							
10							
11							
12							
13							
14							
15							
16							
17							
18							
19							
20							
21							
22							
23	3. Total, Items 1 & 2						
24	4. Item 6 minus Item 3*						
25							
26	5. Variable Expenses:						
27							
28							
29							
30							
31							
32							
33							
34							
35							
36	6. Spendable Income						
37							
38	Notes: For all items, check-off (✓) when paid.						
39	For periodic budget items, enter months due-example (1,3,6).						
40	* Monthly amount available for variable expenses.						

Budget of Cash, Expenses, and Income

National ® Brand   45-606   Eye-Ease ®
                    45-306   2 - Pack
                    Made in USA   NAME: _____   YEAR: _____ | | Initials | Date |
                                                                               |---|---|---|
                                                                               | Prepared By | | |

BUDGET OF CASH, EXPENSES, AND INCOME | Approved By | | |

	BUDGET ITEM	(✓) JULY	(✓) AUG	(✓) SEPT	(✓) OCT	(✓) NOV	(✓) DEC	
1	1. Cash – 1st – Half							1
2	Cash – 2nd – Half							2
3	2. Recurring Expenses:							3
4								4
5								5
6								6
7								7
8								8
9								9
10								10
11								11
12								12
13								13
14								14
15								15
16								16
17								17
18								18
19								19
20								20
21								21
22								22
23	3. Total, Items 1 & 2							23
24	4. Item 6 minus Item 3*							24
25								25
26	5. Variable Expenses							26
27								27
28								28
29								29
30								30
31								31
32								32
33								33
34								34
35								35
36	6. Spendable Income							36
37								37
38	Notes: For all items, check-off (✓) when paid.							38
39	For periodic budget items, enter month due – example (7,9,11)							39
40	* Monthly amount available for variable expenses.							40

National ®Brand 45-606 Eye-Ease®
45-306 2 - Pack
Made in USA NAME: _____ YEAR: _____

	Initials	Date
Prepared By		
Approved By		

ACTUAL EXPENSE PAYMENTS – RECURRING AND VARIABLE

	PAYEE (MONTH DUE)	JAN (*)	FEB (*)	MAR (*)	APR (*)	MAY (*)	JUNE (*)	
		AMOUNT AND DATE PAID						
1	Recurring Expenses:							1
2								2
3								3
4								4
5								5
6								6
7								7
8								8
9								9
10								10
11								11
12								12
13								13
14								14
15								15
16								16
17								17
18								18
19								19
20								20
21								21
22								22
23								23
24								24
25								25
26	Variable Expenses:							26
27								27
28								28
29								29
30								30
31								31
32								32
33								33
34								34
35								35
36								36
37								37
38								38
39	* (Date paid)							39
40								40

Actual Expense Payments – Recurring and Variable

National® Brand   45-606   Eye-Ease®
45-306   2 - Pack
Made in USA   NAME: _____   YEAR: _____

ACTUAL EXPENSE PAYMENTS – RECURRING AND VARIABLE

| | | | Prepared By | Initials | Date |
| | | | Approved By | | |

	PAYEE (MONTH DUE)	JULY (*)	AUG (*)	SEPT (*)	OCT (*)	NOV (*)	DEC (*)	
		1	2	AMOUNT AND DATE PAID 3	4	5	6	
1	Recurring Expenses:							1
2								2
3								3
4								4
5								5
6								6
7								7
8								8
9								9
10								10
11								11
12								12
13								13
14								14
15								15
16								16
17								17
18								18
19								19
20								20
21								21
22								22
23								23
24								24
25								25
26	Variable Expenses:							26
27								27
28								28
29								29
30								30
31								31
32								32
33								33
34								34
35								35
36								36
37								37
38								38
39	* (Date paid)							39
40								40

National Brand 45-606 Eye-Ease 45-306 2 - Pack Made in USA

NAME: YEAR:

	Initials	Date
Prepared By		
Approved By		

ACTUAL EXPENSE PAYMENTS - MEDICAL, DENTAL, AND MISCELLANEOUS

			1	2	3	4	5	6	
			AMOUNT PAID				NOTES		
	DATE	PAYEE	MEDICAL	DENTAL	MISC.				
1									1
2									2
3									3
4									4
5									5
6									6
7									7
8									8
9									9
10									10
11									11
12									12
13									13
14									14
15									15
16									16
17									17
18									18
19									19
20									20
21									21
22									22
23									23
24									24
25									25
26									26
27									27
28									28
29									29
30									30
31									31
32									32
33									33
34									34
35									35
36									36
37									37
38									38
39									39
40									40

Actual Expense Payments – Medical, Dental, and Miscellaneous

HOME SWEET WELL MANAGED HOME

National® Brand 45-606 Eye-Ease®
45-306 2 - Pack
Made in USA

NAME: _____   YEAR: _____

	Initials	Date
Prepared By		
Approved By		

CALCULATION OF HOUSEHOLD FINANCIAL POSITION

A. SHORT TERM POSITION

TODAYS DATE: _____   POSITION DATE: _____

AMOUNT

1. Cash on hand today
2. Add checking account balance today (from register)
3. Add income expected from today through position date
4. Total amount available – sum of Items 1, 2, and 3

For the period from today through the position date:
5. Subtract unpaid recurring expense budget items
6. Subtract unpaid estimated variable expenses
7. Subtract other known planned expenditures
8. Total of subtracted Items 5, 6, and 7

9. Unassigned net amount on position date (Item 4 less Item 8)

B. LONG TERM POSITION (USE WHOLE MONTH AMOUNTS ONLY)

AMOUNT

Evaluation Period (start and end months):

1. Total spendable income
2. Total budgeted cash and recurring expenses
3. Total available for variable (controllable) expenses*

* College funds, savings, credit purchases, reserves, or other
  discretionary expenditures.

Calculation of Household Financial Position

136

National® Brand 45-606 Eye-Ease®
45-306 2 - Pack
Made in USA

NAME: _____ YEAR: _____

	Initial's	Date
Prepared By		
Approved By		

ESTIMATED SPENDABLE INCOME

	SOURCE OF INCOME	JAN	FEB	MAR	APR	MAY	JUNE	
1								1
2	Salary/Wages:							2
3	First							3
4	Second							4
5	Commissions							5
6	Bonus							6
7	Company Pension:							7
8	First							8
9	Second							9
10	Social Security:							10
11	First							11
12	Second							12
13	401 K Proceeds:							13
14	First							14
15	Second							15
16	Interest (Bonds,Banks,etc)							16
17	Dividends (Stocks,Funds)							17
18	Rentals							18
19	Trust Proceeds							19
20	Other:							20
21	First							21
22	Second							22
23	Third							23
24	Fourth							24
25								25
26								26
27								27
28								28
29								29
30								30
31	TOTAL:							31
32								32
33								33
34								34
35								35
36	Note: Enter monthly totals in the Income section of the Budget of							36
37	Cash, Expenses, and Income form.							37
38								38
39								39
40								40

Estimated Spendable Income

HOME SWEET WELL MANAGED HOME

NAME: _____   YEAR: _____

	Initials	Date
Prepared By		
Approved By		

ESTIMATED SPENDABLE INCOME

	SOURCE OF INCOME	JULY	AUG	SEPT	OCT	NOV	DEC	
1								1
2	Salary/Wages:							2
3	First							3
4	Second							4
5	Commissions							5
6	Bonus							6
7	Company Pension:							7
8	First							8
9	Second							9
10	Social Security:							10
11	First							11
12	Second							12
13	401 K Proceeds:							13
14	First							14
15	Second							15
16	Interest (Bonds,Bank,etc)							16
17	Dividends (Stocks,Funds)							17
18	Rentals							18
19	Trust Proceeds							19
20	Other:							20
21	First							21
22	Second							22
23	Third							23
24	Fourth							24
25								25
26								26
27								27
28								28
29								29
30								30
31	TOTAL:							31
32								32
33								33
34								34
35								35
36	Note: Enter monthly totals in the Income section of the Budget of							36
37	Cash, Expenses, and Income form.							37
38								38
39								39
40								40

Estimated Spendable Income

National ®Brand 45-606 Eye-Ease®
45-306 2 - Pack
Made in USA

			NAME:			Prepared By	Initials / Date
			MASTER INVESTMENT RECORD			Approved By	

	NO.	INVESTMENTS					PAGE				
1		Description:									1
2		Date Purchased & Broker Name:									2
3		Total Amount Paid & Source of Funds:									3
4		Where Applicable, Interest Rate & Maturity Date:									4
5		Date Sold, Sale Price, & Use of Proceeds:									5
6											6
7											7
8											8
9		Description:									9
10		Date Purchased & Broker Name:									10
11		Total Amount Paid & Source of Funds:									11
12		Where Applicable Interest Rate & Maturity Date:									12
13		Date Sold, Sale Price & Use of Proceeds:									13
14											14
15											15
16											16
17		Description:									17
18		Date Purchased & Broker Name:									18
19		Total Amount Paid & Source of Funds:									19
20		Where Applicable Interest Rate & Maturity Date:									20
21		Date Sold, Sale Price & Use of Proceeds:									21
22											22
23											23
24											24
25		Description:									25
26		Date Purchased & Broker Name:									26
27		Total Amount Paid & Source of Funds:									27
28		Where Applicable Interest Rate & Maturity Date:									28
29		Date Sold, Sale Price & Use of Proceeds:									29
30											30
31											31
32											32
33		Description:									33
34		Date Purchased & Broker Name:									34
35		Total Amount Paid & Source of Funds:									35
36		Where Applicable Interest Rate & Maturity Date:									36
37		Date Sold, Sale Price & Use of Proceeds:									37
38											38
39											39
40											40

Master Investment Record

DURABLE POWER OF ATTORNEY FOR HEALTH CARE DECISIONS

1. CREATION OF DURABLE POWER OF ATTORNEY FOR HEALTH CARE

By this document I intend to create a durable power of attorney by appointing the person designated below to make health care decisions for me as allowed by Sections 2410 to 2444, inclusive, of the ⋅   This power of attorney shall not be affected by my subsequent incapacity. I hereby revoke any prior durable power of attorney for health care. I am a ⋅ who is at least 18 years old, of sound mind, and acting of my own free will.

2. APPOINTMENT OF HEALTH CARE AGENT

(Fill in below the name, address and telephone number of the person you wish to make health care decisions for you if you become incapacitated. You should make sure that this person agrees to accept this responsibility. The following may not serve as your agent: (1) your treating health care provider; (2) an operator of a community care facility or residential care facility for the elderly; or (3) an employee of your treating health care provider, a community care facility, or a residential care facility for the elderly, unless that employee is related to you by blood, marriage or adoption. If you are a conservatee under the Lanterman-Petris-Short Act (the law governing involuntary commitment to a mental health facility) and you wish to appoint your conservator as your agent, you must consult a lawyer, who must sign and attach a special declaration for this document to be valid.)

I, _____ , hereby appoint:
　　　　　　　　(insert your name)

Name _____

Address _____

Work Telephone (_____) _____   Home Telephone (_____) _____

as my agent (attorney-in-fact) to make health care decisions for me as authorized in this document. I understand that this power of attorney will be effective for an indefinite period of time unless I revoke it or limit its duration below.

(Optional) This power of attorney shall expire on the following date: _____ .

ǀ

Durable Power of Attorney for Health Care Decisions

3. AUTHORITY OF AGENT

If I become incapable of giving informed consent to health care decisions, I grant my agent full power and authority to make those decisions for me, subject to any statements of desires or limitations set forth below. Unless I have limited my agent's authority in this document, that authority shall include the right to consent, refuse consent, or withdraw consent to any medical care, treatment, service, or procedure; to receive and to consent to the release of medical information; to authorize an autopsy to determine the cause of my death; to make a gift of all or part of my body; and to direct the disposition of my remains, subject to any instructions I have given in a written contract for funeral services, my will or by some other method. I understand that, by law, my agent may **not** consent to any of the following: commitment to a mental health treatment facility, convulsive treatment, psychosurgery, sterilization or abortion.

4. MEDICAL TREATMENT DESIRES AND LIMITATIONS (OPTIONAL)

(Your agent must make health care decisions that are consistent with your known desires. You may, but are not required to, state your desires about the kinds of medical care you do or do not want to receive, including your desires concerning life support if you are seriously ill. If you do not want your agent to have the authority to make certain decisions, you must write a statement to that effect in the space provided below; otherwise, your agent will have the broad powers to make health care decisions for you that are outlined in paragraph 3 above. In either case, it is important that you discuss your health care desires with the person you appoint as your agent and with your doctor(s).)

(Following is a general statement about withholding and removal of life-sustaining treatment. If the statement accurately reflects your desires, you may initial it. If you wish to add to it or to write your own statement instead, you may do so in the space provided.)

> I do **not** want efforts made to prolong my life and I do **not** want life-sustaining treatment to be provided or continued: (1) if I am in an irreversible coma or persistent vegetative state; or (2) if I am terminally ill and the use of life-sustaining procedures would serve only to artificially delay the moment of my death; or (3) under any other circumstances where the burdens of the treatment outweigh the expected benefits. In making decisions about life-sustaining treatment under provision (3) above, I want my agent to consider the relief of suffering and the quality of my life, as well as the extent of the possible prolongation of my life.
>
> *If this statement reflects your desires, initial here:* _____

Other or additional statements of medical treatment desires and limitations: _____

_____

_____

_____

_____

(You may attach additional pages if you need more space to complete your statements. Each additional page must be dated and signed at the same time you date and sign this document.)

5. APPOINTMENT OF ALTERNATE AGENTS (OPTIONAL)

(You may appoint alternate agents to make health care decisions for you in case the person you appointed in Paragraph 2 is unable or unwilling to do so.)

If the person named as my agent in Paragraph 2 is not available or willing to make health care decisions for me as authorized in this document, I appoint the following persons to do so, listed in the order they should be asked:

First Alternate Agent: Name _____   Work Telephone (_____) _____

Address _____   Home Telephone (_____) _____

Second Alternate Agent: Name_____   Work Telephone (_____) _____

Address _____   Home Telephone (_____) _____

6. USE OF COPIES

I hereby authorize that photocopies of this document can be relied upon by my agent and others as though they were originals.

2

DATE AND SIGNATURE OF PRINCIPAL
(You must date and sign this power of attorney)

I sign my name to this Durable Power of Attorney for Health Care at _____, _____
(City) (State)

on _____. _____
(Date) (Signature of Principal)

STATEMENT OF WITNESSES

(This power of attorney will not be valid for making health care decisions unless it is either (1) signed by two qualified adult witnesses who personally know you (or to whom you present evidence of your identity) and who are present when you sign or acknowledge your signature or (2) acknowledged before a notary public in   If you elect to use witnesses rather than a notary public, the law provides that none of the following may be used as witnesses: (1) the persons you have appointed as your agent and alternate agents; (2) your health care provider or an employee of your health care provider; or (3) an operator or employee of an operator of a community care facility or residential care facility for the elderly. Additionally, at least one of the witnesses cannot be related to you by blood, marriage or adoption, or be named in your will. IF YOU ARE A PATIENT IN A SKILLED NURSING FACILITY, YOU MUST HAVE A PATIENT ADVOCATE OR OMBUDSMAN SIGN BOTH THE STATEMENT OF WITNESSES BELOW AND THE DECLARATION ON THE FOLLOWING PAGE.)

I declare under penalty of perjury under the laws of   that the person who signed or acknowledged this document is personally known to me to be the principal, or that the identity of the principal was proved to me by convincing evidence;* that the principal signed or acknowledged this durable power of attorney in my presence, that the principal appears to be of sound mind and under no duress, fraud, or undue influence; that I am not the person appointed as attorney in fact by this document; and that I am not the principal's health care provider, an employee of the principal's health care provider, the operator of a community care facility or a residential care facility for the elderly, nor an employee of an operator of a community care facility or residential care facility for the elderly.

Signature _____   Signature _____

Print name _____   Print name _____

Date _____   Date _____

Residence Address _____   Residence Address_____

_____   _____

(AT LEAST ONE OF THE ABOVE WITNESSES MUST ALSO SIGN THE FOLLOWING DECLARATION)

I further declare under penalty of perjury under the laws of   that I am not related to the principal by blood, marriage, or adoption, and, to the best of my knowledge I am not entitled to any part of the estate of the principal upon the death of the principal under a will now existing or by operation of law.

Signature: _____

*The law allows one or more of the following forms of identification as convincing evidence of identity: a   driver's license or identification card or U.S. passport that is current or has been issued within five years, or any of the following if the document is current or has been issued within five years, contains a photograph and description of the person named on it, is signed by the person, and bears a serial or other identifying number: a foreign passport that has been stamped by the U.S. Immigration and Naturalization Service; a driver's license issued by another state or by an authorized Canadian or Mexican agency; or an identification card issued by another state or by any branch of the U.S. armed forces. If the principal is a patient in a skilled nursing facility, a patient advocate or ombudsman may rely on the representations of family members or the administrator or staff of the facility as convincing evidence of identity if the patient advocate or ombudsman believes that the representations provide a reasonable basis for determining the identity of the principal.

3

Date and Signature of Principal

HOME SWEET WELL MANAGED HOME

Special Requirement: Statement of Patient Advocate or Ombudsman

---

SPECIAL REQUIREMENT: STATEMENT OF PATIENT ADVOCATE OR OMBUDSMAN

(If you are a patient in a skilled nursing facility, a patient advocate or ombudsman must sign the Statement of Witnesses above and must also sign the following declaration.)

I further declare under penalty of perjury under the laws of _____ that I am a patient advocate or ombudsman as designated by the State Department of Aging and am serving as a witness as required by subdivision (f) of Civil Code Section 2432.

Signature: _____   Address: _____

Print Name: _____   _____

Date: _____   _____

CERTIFICATE OF ACKNOWLEDGMENT OF NOTARY PUBLIC

(Acknowledgment before a notary public is __not__ required if you have elected to have two qualified witnesses sign above. If you are a patient in a skilled nursing facility, you __must__ have a patient advocate or ombudsman sign the Statement of Witnesses on page 3 __and__ the Statement of Patient Advocate or Ombudsman above)

)
)ss.
County of _____)

On this _____ day of _____, in the year _____,

before me, _____,
                        (here insert name and title of the officer)

personally appeared _____
                                (here insert name of principal)

personally known to me (or proved to me on the basis of satisfactory evidence) to be the person whose name is subscribed to this instrument, and acknowledged to me that he or she executed the same in his or her authorized capacity, and that by his or her signature on the instrument the person executed the instrument.

WITNESS my hand and official seal.

_____
        (Signature of Notary Public)

                                                            NOTARY SEAL

COPIES

YOUR AGENT MAY NEED THIS DOCUMENT IMMEDIATELY IN CASE OF AN EMERGENCY. YOU SHOULD KEEP THE COMPLETED ORIGINAL AND GIVE PHOTOCOPIES OF THE COMPLETED ORIGINAL TO (1) YOUR AGENT AND ALTERNATE AGENTS, (2) YOUR PERSONAL PHYSICIAN, AND (3) MEMBERS OF YOUR FAMILY AND ANY OTHER PERSONS WHO MIGHT BE CALLED IN THE EVENT OF A MEDICAL EMERGENCY. THE LAW PERMITS THAT PHOTOCOPIES OF THE COMPLETED DOCUMENT CAN BE RELIED UPON AS THOUGH THEY WERE ORIGINALS.

4

BIBLIOGRAPHY

Hartford Underwriters Insurance Company – Security, Safety, and Insurance, 2003
The Holy Bible, New International Version
Living Trusts, John C. Roberts, Attorney at Law, 2002

Printed in the United States
by Baker & Taylor Publisher Services